THE S

The Survivors

The story of the Belsen remnant

Told by
LESLIE H. HARDMAN
and written by
CECEILY GOODMAN

Foreword by
The Rt. Hon. LORD RUSSELL OF LIVERPOOL

VALLENTINE MITCHELL
LONDON • PORTLAND, OR

First published in 1958 by Vallentine Mitchell

Suite 314, Premier House,   920 NE 58th Avenue, Suite 300
112–114 Station Road,   Portland, Oregon,
Edgware, Middlesex   97213-3786,
HA8 7BJ, UK   USA

www.vmbooks.com

Copyright © 1958 Leslie H. Hardman and Cecily Goodman
reprinted 2009

British Library Cataloguing in Publication Data

Hardman, Leslie H.
The survivors : the story of the Belsen remnant
1. Hardman, Leslie H. 2. Great Britain. Army - Chaplains -
Biography 3. Bergen-Belsen (Concentration camp) 4. Military
chaplains - Judaism - Biography 5. World War, 1939-1945 -
Chaplains - Biography 6. World War, 1939-1945 -
Concentration camps - Liberation - Germany 7. Concentration
camp inmates - Germany - Social conditions 8. Holocaust
survivors - Germany - Social conditions
I. Title II. Goodman, Cecily
940.5'31853595'092

ISBN 978 0 85303 831 3 (cloth)
ISBN 978 0 85303 821 4 (paper)

Library of Congress Cataloging-in-Publication Data:
A catalog record has been applied for

*All rights reserved. No part of this publication may be reproduced,
stored in or introduced into a retrieval system, or transmitted, in any
form or by any means, electronic, mechanical, photocopying,
recording or otherwise, without the prior written permission of the
publisher of this book.*

Printed by The Good News Press Ltd, Ongar, Essex

CONTENTS

ILLUSTRATIONS

ACKNOWLEDGMENTS

The authors express their indebtedness to the Rt. Hon. Lord Russell of Liverpool, C.B.E., M.C. for his kindness in writing the foreword. They also thank the Imperial War Museum for granting permission to reproduce the photographs in this book, Mr Joshua Shindler for permission to use the translation of 'The Partisans' Song', and Mr H. C. Stevens for his great help in the course of production.

FOREWORD

by the Rt. Hon. LORD RUSSELL OF LIVERPOOL, c.b.e., m.c.

So many books have been written about the German concentration camps that it may be wondered whether there is room for yet another; but no one who reads the account of what the Rev. Leslie Hardman found in Belsen immediately after its liberation by British troops on 15th April 1945 will have any doubt of the answer.

This book is different.

It is told by the Jewish Chaplain with a British unit stationed at Celle who was sent by his C.O. to Belsen with these words: 'Keep a stiff upper lip Padre, we've just been into Belsen concentration camp, and it's horrible; but you have got to go there; you'll find a lot of your people.'

This book is the story of what the Chaplain found when he got there and of the difficulties and problems which had to be faced.

There were many of the inmates who were beyond all human help, but the majority of those who were not already beyond recall eventually regained the will to live.

There is a persistent school of thought, which to me is entirely misguided, that German war crimes should be forgotten. Forgiven, maybe, though that must take some time, and the measure of forgiveness should surely be, to some degree, in proportion to the criminals' repentance.

But there can be no real forgiveness without full knowledge; 'to know all is to forgive all.'

That is the golden thread which runs through this entire book.

An attempt was made by Hitler to exterminate all the

Jews in Europe and it was only circumvented by the Allies winning the war when they did. It was to be 'the final solution of the Jewish problem'.

No one could be surprised were the few survivors of this genocide found to be incapable of any measure of forgiveness. But most of them did not feel like that. Their national conscience would not let them.

Let a little boy, an inmate of the camp, and only fourteen years old at the time of the liberation speak for them all.

He met Mr Hardman one day as he was entering the camp and was asked by the Chaplain where he had been.

'I have been walking about the streets,' he said, 'and I was not molested. . . . I saw German children playing outside their houses but I couldn't kill them, I couldn't even hit them.'

The Chaplain asked him what he meant.

'Haven't you heard of the gas chambers?' the boy asked. 'Haven't you heard of the crematoria? Haven't you heard how we were dragged from our homes, beaten and kicked in the streets? Do you not know that they murdered my parents?'

The Chaplain said he knew all that.

'Well,' said the boy, 'children like those I saw in the street today used to beat us and kick us, then laugh and spit on us. But I couldn't do that to them, I just couldn't do it, my Jewish conscience wouldn't permit me.'

CHAPTER ONE

'ABANDON HOPE...'

THE DAY AFTER the entry of the British troops into Belsen on April 15th, 1945, I returned from Holland to my regimental headquarters at Celle. When I arrived I was greeted with a brooding, heavy stillness; over everything was an ominous hush. I went into the mess and found several officers, all of them strangely quiet. They greeted me in silence. I asked,

'What's happening? What's wrong? – there seems to be a peculiar feeling . . .'

One of them came over to me; he said reluctantly:

'We've uncovered a concentration camp.'

He turned his head away, but not before I caught the pity in his eyes.

The Colonel sent for me, and I went with a stone instead of a heart. I found him grim and white-faced; something had changed him too.

'Keep a stiff upper lip, Padre,' he said. 'We've just been into Belsen concentration camp, and it's horrible; but you have got to go there; you'll find a lot of your people. It's too late to go now, go tomorrow morning.'

The following morning I went by car from Celle to Belsen, some twelve miles' distance. I drove at reckless speed, and yet I felt that my truck was moving at a snail's pace. By this time I had steeled my nerves to pin-pointing my thoughts on how soon I could reach my people, how soon I could do something for them.

As I drew closer to the camp, before reaching the gate I saw nailed on almost every tree the warning sign, 'Danger

– Typhus'. As I got out of the truck I had a sense of shock; I knew I should have anticipated it, but to be faced suddenly with that dreaded disease enveloped me in a chill which was almost paralysing. I did not need to be reminded of the Colonel's words:

'A lot of your people are there.'

I showed my pass to the two British Tommies guarding the entrance, and walked into Belsen Camp.

I shall always remember the first person I met. It was a girl, and I thought she was a negress. Her face was dark brown, and I afterwards learnt that this was because her skin was in the process of healing, after being burnt. When she saw me she made as though to throw her arms around me; but with the instinct of self-preservation, I jumped back. Instantly I felt ashamed; but she understood, and stood away from me.

I looked at her; fear, compassion and shame were struggling for mastery within me; but she was the more composed of the two. We walked into the compound, keeping our voluntary 'no-man's-land' between us. Suddenly my body stiffened, and I stood still in my tracks. Before and around me were lying dozens of emaciated bodies, naked, semi-naked, huddled together.

'Are they all asleep?' I asked.

'No, they're dead; they've been there for days,' the girl replied unemotionally, stating the simple fact.

I tried to look at them again. I had to look in order to know, to learn, and if possible to help; but these were beyond help: these, my people. The foul stench which polluted the air sickened me, and only the girl's presence enabled me to overcome my nausea.

As we walked on, towards us came what seemed to me to be the remnants of a holocaust – a tottering mass of blackened skin and bones, held together somehow with filthy rags.

'My God, the dead are walking!' I cried aloud, but I did not recognise my voice.

'They are not dead,' said the girl. 'But they soon will be.'

To give you a clearer picture of what I found on that day, I must go back to February 1945, as described in the words of a Belsen prisoner, Dr Leo Fritz, in April.

* * *

'Three months ago a long column of men shuffled from the Camp Sachsenhausen to the "Sick Camp" Bergen-Belsen. There were three thousand of us, sick and healthy, and eight of us were doctors. When we started out it was raining heavily, but we took with us the hope that where we were going our miserable existence would become just about bearable. How was it that we, who had suffered so much, still retained any illusions?

'We had only the vague information passed on by those who had been engaged in building the camps, and who had spoken of satisfactory sanitation; over the past two or three years there had been a gradual but perceptible change in the various compounds. For the past nine months the transports to the gas chambers at Lublin had stopped; instead the cases of chronic and prolonged illness were being removed to the sick bay at Belsen. In the concentration camps many of the internees fell ill owing to the heavy work, fatigues, bad food and beatings; medical treatment was wholly inadequate, and the possibility of healing almost hopeless. Under the supervision of an SS doctor only unskilled internees were permitted to treat the sick. The sick bays overflowed; but this problem the SS solved simply enough – they "removed" the sick inmates. Tuberculosis sufferers were frequently taken to Lublin, to perish in the gas chambers.

'Then Germany experienced a great shortage of labour; "K.Z." slaves were in demand. In many concentration camps the conditions grew easier. Beatings were less severe, internees were allowed to receive parcels so that they should be better fed, some were given permission to let their cropped hair grow again, and in certain camps cinemas, and even brothels were opened. Internee doctors were used in the sick bays, for now the sick must recover as soon as possible. Their capacity for labour had become more important than their capacity for degradation.

'So the transports to Lublin were stopped, and were replaced by transfers to the "Sick Camp" Bergen-Belsen. This slight alleviation of the former dire inhumanity found us still human enough to believe that at Belsen a fair number of those with chronic ailments would recover. But we had yet to sound the fiendish depths to which man can descend when he sinks below the level of the beast.

'When we arrived at Belsen, we found even the elements as pitiless as our jailers. As we waited in front of the ramshackle barracks which were to be our new home it rained heavily – and we had to wait a very long time.

'Wet, cold, sick, miserable, we at length entered our new abode – several barracks approximately fifty yards long, with doors and windows missing, an ice-cold wind blowing through the openings and the rain coming through the roofs and forming large pools of water on the floor. There was no furniture whatsoever. Some straw was scattered about; it was already partly wet, and soon was so wet as to be useless. Everybody camped down on the floorboards, we were packed like sardines; from seven to eight thousand men were pushed into a single barrack.

'During the first few days we were given some bread, although very little, and watery turnip soup, which we swallowed down greedily. There were neither tools nor materials for repairing the damage to windows, walls and roofs, and hard as we tried during the first few weeks, everything was refused us. Only by thieving and bribery were we able to obtain shovels, hammers, and, later on, some roofing felt.

'Any possibility of medical treatment for the many thousand sick cases was out of the question. During those first few weeks people with high temperatures, tuberculosis, mutilations, and open wounds, were lying together on the floor. There were no bandages, no medical supplies: nothing at all. There was only the daily roll call, which lasted about three or four hours – sometimes longer. Day after day, in ice-cold wind and rain the sick stood and waited until the many thousands were counted and accounted for. Day after day, many dropped down, never to get up again. The weak ones were dragged into a special block, the notorious Block 15, where they were exposed to slow death. On one side of this block was the great mortuary. Before it lay the dead; in front of them the half dead and dying; then those so weak they could no longer crawl; and finally those who were rather better. The whole process was just like a horrible conveyor belt. At first you were well up in front; but in a few days, pushed by other bodies, dragged by the room orderlies, you had reached the death chamber.

'Some days after our arrival we were given three small rooms to be used as a sick bay; except for plenty of dirt and rubbish, they were empty. During the next few days we doctors removed the dirt by the cubic yard; somewhere we found a few ramshackle and broken beds, which we repaired and carried into the sick bay. "Beds" is hardly a fitting word, as they were wooden structures with a blanket or two; there were no mattresses, no sheets, no straw. Eventually the small rooms were ready to receive the sick; then a few medicines arrived. It was impossible to accept all the many thousand sick people into the ward; there was room for only four hundred, allotting one small bed for two men. Such were the conditions provided for people who through hunger had become human skeletons. There were no towels. Water was scarce; it was turned off for days on end. Cleanliness was all important to us, as many of the sick were suffering from diarrhoea, the result of the turnip soup. We tried to keep the place clean, but the people were so weak with hunger they could not carry on. Hunger was becoming the greatest menace in the camp. We were issued less and less bread. Then came days without any bread at all. People fell like flies, and we had many hundred deaths a day. Sometimes over a thousand.

'The SS then decided to transfer all the overworked, the weak and the sick from all the other concentration camps to Bergen-Belsen. So they arrived in large transports, often amounting to many thousands. They came mostly by train – seventy or a hundred in one truck, packed together tightly for many days, and often without food or drink. They were transferred to lorries, and when they reached the camp they came tumbling out. Hundreds of them arrived dead, already turning green and decomposing. Those who were alive could hardly walk or crawl. Our camp was filled again with masses of people who desperately needed help, but for whom our resources for help were terribly, terribly small. It was hard, wanting to help and not being able to do so. When we walked through the barracks, hundreds of supplicating hands were outstretched, we heard hundreds of calls for help, but there was room for only two or three more in the sick quarters. Day and night we saw and heard the people near to death, pushing and stepping on one another, crying and sobbing, fighting for places. Day and night it was impossible to get to sleep.

'It was then that cannibalism started in the camp. It began in barrack 10, one of the worst starvation barracks, where a special party was kept because of the danger of an outbreak of typhus. In this barrack was found a corpse which had been cut open and the liver torn out. During the next few days there were five or six similar incidents. The corpses lay about outside and inside the barracks, and the people cut off ears, cheeks, and later, when the cannibals could not get enough, they took parts of the arm and leg muscles and buttocks. Even the genitals were taken. Sometimes one of these cannibals was caught eating or cooking human flesh. The SS ordered that these miserable and starving creatures were to be beaten to death, and there was always someone brutal enough to carry out the order. But even so there were hundreds of these degraded, wretched and famished people of all nationalities and ages, who in their desperation tried to prolong their lives in this way.

'Another punishment was to force the unhappy wretch to take out a dead man's eye, hold it between his lips and remain in a sitting position with hands stretched above his head for two hours. At the slightest sign of weakness causing him to lower his hands he was beaten viciously until he expired.

'The other plague was the lice. As there was barely an opportunity to wash, the camp was hopelessly overcrowded and a bath or a change of clothes was impossible, the place gradually became lice-ridden. We were tormented by hundreds and even thousands of lice; we said our clothes could walk around by themselves! We had no means to destroy the pests; there was only one remedy: to crush them with the fingers. And so they did, as well as they could. Often we saw people rubbing their backs against the corner of the huts, in order to ease the incessant itching caused by the bites. Most of the prisoners were covered with open sores, their skin was red and blood-stained. These sores, caused by endless scratching, developed into boils and ulcers. Very rarely did we see anyone with a clean skin. And then came what we had been dreading for some time – typhus. It was brought in from another camp, began with one or two isolated cases, and then spread like wildfire. Frequently it could not even be diagnosed, as the prisoners were packed tightly together and examination was impossible. It was just as impossible to find room for them in the two barracks reserved for typhus patients. The sick bay, lice-ridden as it had become, was a hotbed of typhus, and all our efforts to check it were in vain. We were without any of the necessary materials, and, much as we pleaded with the SS doctors, nothing drastic was done. Hundreds and hundreds of typhus cases passed through our hands, and our medical work increased. There was only one hope – the approach of the warmer season, when the lice would die out. But meanwhile we lost many of our best comrades. Of the men who were infected, a quarter died; there was almost the same percentage among the women cases.

'During March 1945 a devilish plan was conceived by the SS. They intended to build, partly underground, a large barracks, which they admitted was to be a "gas chamber". The plan was ready, the builders were ordered, the time estimated for completion was four or five weeks. We knew that the British had reached the Rhine, and those of us who knew also of the latest SS plan for our extermination feverishly counted the days as the front line approached. It was a race with time. Which would reach us first? We heard the distant thunder of the guns. Would they arrive before the gas?

'At that time the corpses in our camp were stacked up in mountainous heaps in front and at the sides of the huts. The clothing had to be burnt separately, so they were all naked, almost skeletons, though sometimes with swollen legs. They turned green and putrescent in the open air, there were no facilities for their removal. At the end of the camp was a small crematorium which worked day and night. The smell of burning flesh polluted the air for days on end. We were frequently forced to close the windows, as we could not stand the pestilential stench. But the crematorium was not able to cope with its tremendous task. So the SS built huge pyres, many yards square, and stacked the bodies high between layers of timber. These pyres were kept burning for days, the smoke rose up to 3,000 feet, and the sickening smell of decay grew even worse. Stench, misery, and heaps of corpses were our daily lot, and we had to use all our mental powers to prevent ourselves becoming apathetic, and even try to improve matters where it was still possible.

'When the British were only a few miles away the SS made a special effort to clean up the camp. Fear suddenly took possession of them!

' "We shall organise a procession," said the SS Rapportführer cynically. The corpses had to be dragged away. There were no stretchers or vehicles, so the survivors had to fasten ropes around the arms and legs of the bodies and haul them away. Each filthy, naked body needed two to four men to pull it, so weak were they. Through the camp they dragged each corpse, through pools of mud, over the stones, past the men's camp, past the women's camp, to dump them in great pits. The traces of this horrible procession were visible all along the route; it went on day after day, slowly, pace by pace. Every day seven hundred bodies were dragged away, and many thousands had yet to be removed. During the last two and a half months, 50,000 people, mainly between twenty and forty years of age, people of all nations, perished from disease and hunger; victims of this hell called "Sick Camp". Among the survivors thousands were merely walking skeletons, and many hundreds more died afterwards.

'But these sick, miserable, degraded, starved and dying prisoners succeeded in caring for 700 children in the camp. There were many babies amongst this number and the children were of various ages, but the prisoners provided for them – the children survived – and to know this was a comfort.

'Then came the miracle of April 15th. The roar of the British tanks and trucks; and at last – at long, long last – liberation.'

*　　*　　*

This was what confronted me on the 17th day of April

1945. I had walked into something a thousand times more appalling than I had steeled myself to meet . . . 'Keep a stiff upper lip, Padre!'

A terrible feeling of helplessness engulfed me. What could I do? How could I save them? Where could I begin? I was a pigmy grappling with a mountain.

'Many of your people are there.' My people? – anyone's people – everyone's people. These once human beings, flesh and blood like you and me, were now reduced to hideous apparitions bearing no resemblance to man, but only witnessing to man's inhumanity.

God help me! I am small and alone but I must help them; and I must not waste a moment, because every moment another soul dies.

CHAPTER TWO

FOOD, FOOD!

I HAVE NO CLEAR IDEA of how much time passed between my meeting the girl with the burnt face and the approach of a military policeman. Was it minutes, hours, or a decade? – Was this a nightmare fashioned out of some strange unknown personal fault of mine? I looked back; I saw again the pile of decaying corpses, a huge rotting mound of human debris, its smell more offensive than that of stagnant vegetation, its sight shattering to the eye, its portent making the mind reel. My mind groped its way slowly and painfully back through the dark passage of Time, out into the abyss of the present.

'You'd better get powdered, sir.'

I looked into the fresh-complexioned, round-cheeked, firm-chinned face of the young soldier. I could read nothing in its pleasant but blank expression. He took me into a little room, which I learnt later was part of a hut which Kramer, the Beast of Belsen, had used as his office. Here I was effectively 'dusted'.

The girl with the brown face had followed me, and waited for me outside. As I came out of the hut she came up and asked: 'Will you come and see a few of my friends?'

Her friends were six or eight women, all from Lithuania and Poland. When I appeared in the doorway they looked at me with a glazed apathy. I was there but they did not see me. Even when I entered their hut and spoke to them, they still seemed unconscious of my presence.

The girl with the brown face had spoken to me in Yiddish, and I spoke to them in the same language. I don't

11

know what I said, but my words had no more effect on them than my appearance. Then the girl pointed to the Magen David* on my tunic, and they came forward cautiously, one by one, and peered. Slowly, almost reluctantly, recognition reached their tired, tormented minds – minds that had endured so much, that had been stretched to breaking point, minds they had had to close in order to survive. One poor creature touched and then stroked the badge of my Faith, and finding that it was real, murmured, 'Rabbiner, Rabbiner'. Now the others crowded around me, touching and stroking my tunic. On the previous day, the day of liberation, they had seen khaki; and when the British entered they had wanted to throw their arms around them; they had hugged the trucks and the tanks. Now they had someone of their own, a Jew like themselves, but free and in a British uniform, come to take them by the hand and lead them out of this inferno.

I expected them to break down, but tears were part of a lost world; under the pitiless, searing heat of sadism their tear ducts had long since dried up and shrivelled.

Their hut contained a table and a few chairs. I sat down among them, and slowly they began to talk.

They told me they were in a better condition than most of the inmates of the camp, being the 'nursing sisters', and therefore a 'privileged' group. They had had access to the kitchens, and had been able to scrounge some food. The hut they were now occupying had been theirs since the previous day. When the British entered they had quickly requisitioned this hut, as well as the table and chairs they were now using. They had appropriated some garments, and were now clothed partly in these and partly in their hideous prison garb.

I spent the whole day with them sitting in their hut. They tried to press food on me, but I would eat nothing. I sat smoking, listening, talking, trying to comfort them.

* The double star, the emblem of Jewry.

They told me something of the horrors they had had to endure, the atrocities that had been perpetrated. Ever since the previous November the normal diet had been turnip and potato soup, plus a small portion of bread issued only to those capable of going to the cookhouse. The sick and weak had to go without. For five days preceding the liberation no food or drink whatever was allowed. The 'privileged' groups also suffered horribly; many of the women were pregnant, and many had seen their children and other members of their families brutally and fiendishly murdered.

I endeavoured to guide their talk into the channels of pre-Hitler days. All the understanding of psychology I had then, I had gained from my training and experience as a Rabbi and a Padre, and I felt that I could help most if I could slacken a little the almost intolerable tension of their sorely afflicted minds; if I could kindle some warmth in their frozen hearts; if I could inject some emotion into their withered bodies.

So I sat there for hours, smoking, talking, listening. I spoke to them of Jewish religion and Jewish life, and one of them broke quaveringly into a few lines of a Hebrew song. The pathos of this attempt was so poignant that I put my head on the table and wept; and then they comforted me.

When the time came for me to leave I remembered that in my truck I had a few boxes of Matzos* left over from the Passover distribution. I told them I would get these for them, and I left the hut and walked towards the camp entrance.

On my way I saw coming towards me two young Tommies, each bearing a heavy sack of potatoes on his shoulder. It had been a warm and sunny day, and at late afternoon the sun was still high in heaven; the shadows it threw on the ground were only just beginning to lengthen; those of

* Unleavened bread: made in biscuit form.

the young soldiers and their sacks cast a shorter and more bulky outline on the hardening mud of the compound.

And then, almost as though they had emerged from the ground itself, or had floated out from the retreating shadows of dark corners, a number of wraithlike creatures came tottering towards us. As they drew closer they made frantic efforts to quicken their feeble pace. Their skeleton arms and legs made jerky, grotesque movements as they forced themselves forward. Their bodies, from their heads to their feet, looked like matchsticks. The two young Tommies, entering the camp for the first time, must have thought they had walked into a supernatural world; all the gruesome and frightening tales they had heard as children – and, not so many years since, they had been children – rose up to greet them; the grisly spectacle which confronted them was too much. They dropped their heavy sacks and fled.

In an instant these human skeletons, whose appearance and approach were more a hallucination than reality, fell upon the sacks and their contents almost like locusts descending upon a field of corn. With queer, inarticulate cries, in voices which were thinner and more reedy than those of children, they fell upon the ground, upon the sacks, upon one another, desperately summoning from God knows where an ounce of their lost strength to gain for themselves a precious, a priceless potato.

Aghast and momentarily stunned I looked down upon them. From the writhing human figures a pair of legs like sticks protruded at right angles. I bent down and pulled gently but firmly; I shoved against the encumbering bodies and brought out a female. She lay on the ground gasping for breath, and looking at her I saw that in years she was a girl. For a few minutes I knelt beside her waiting for her to recover; then I picked her up; and she was so light, I thought I had lifted her not with my hands, but only with my compassion.

She stood on her feet, swaying a little. She had no consciousness of me.

The human wraiths had somehow or other disentangled themselves, and were now propelling themselves back from where they had come. I looked at the ground where the potatoes had fallen; apart from scattered pieces of torn sacking, there was nothing left.

The girl gave a thin, shrill cry: then she tottered after the retreating spectres.

I went to my truck and fished out the boxes of Matzos. I was considerably shaken, but took a firm grasp of myself as I once more entered the women's hut. The rapturous welcome they gave both me and my gift was balm to my jangled nerves. When I told them I must leave, they begged me to stay. After many protests I tore myself away, promising to return on the morrow.

Slowly I drove back to Celle, and went straight to my room. There I sank into a fit of deep depression; but, although I was almost prostrate with physical, mental and spiritual shock and exhaustion, I could not rest. I took up pen and paper and wrote down all I had seen and heard that day. When I had finished I went to the window, and, opening it wide, looked out into the night.

There was a world made by God, and I could think only of the world made by Man.

I dropped on to my bed, my body a plaster-cast, my brain a sledge-hammer. But sleep, in her mercy, found me and enfolded me.

CHAPTER THREE

FIRST PRAYERS

As I DROVE to the camp the following morning I realised that it called for two imperative tasks: to get the sick to hospital, and to bury the dead. On arrival I found that the latter task was already being tackled.

A large bulldozer was at work. Open-jawed, it had bitten into the earth, and had eaten out a pit large enough to hold 5,000 bodies. Now, its jaws closed, it thrust its enormous snub nose into the mound of corpses, pushing, pushing it towards the edge of the pit; almost like a dog with its nose to the ground, pushing a heap of bones to a hole it had made, but finding the bones fetid, giving a last sniff and a growl, and backing away.

I went up to the officer in charge of the burial operations. Two SS men were working under his instructions. As the corpses were pushed to the edge of the pit, they took what bodies they could grasp – bodies interlocked, coagulated, disintegrated – and threw them into the huge open wound which was to be the common grave. As I looked down on those poor pitiful bodies, a great sadness came over me. Man returns to dust, but must he return like refuse thrown into a bin?

I turned to the officer in charge. 'Is it not possible to show some reverence to the dead?'

'Padre, I deeply regret it, but we must bury them as quickly as possible; apart from the ghastly sight, there is the danger of disease.' His voice was gentle with understanding, and I knew that something of my bitter sadness had reached him. 'We shall let you know when we have finished,' he said. 'Come back then; you will wish to say some prayers, I'm sure.'

As I walked away I noticed that some of the inmates had come out of their huts and were watching the proceedings. They stood immobile, showing as much interest as we would in the weekly salvage collection. Death had been for so long their constant and close companion that what they now saw moved them not at all.

I proceeded across the compound, intending to make my way to the women's hut I had visited the previous day. Suddenly I was surrounded by a mob of screaming women; their sudden onslaught reminded me of a flock of cackling geese. I saw and heard only the noise and confusion, and could make nothing of what they were trying to tell me. Exerting all my patience, I at length managed to calm them sufficiently and get some sense out of their jumbled cries and screams.

The British Unit had allocated officers to various duties: for sickness, law and order, food, drink, garments, shoes, letter-writing, and so on. There was to be no more 're-quisitioning', and everyone who wanted anything had first to obtain a note or a 'chit' from the officer in charge. Of course these women wanted everything, and their demands had been instantly met with all the necessary 'chits'; but a chit was a note of authority, and for them authority spelt only terror. Then the news reached them that a rabbi from England was in the camp, and this changed the situation completely. He was not the man in uniform, he was their brother; he did not signify authority, he presaged succour; he was not the officer in command, he was their saviour; and a 'chit' from him was a passport to freedom.

I found myself tearing sheet after sheet out of my note-book and handing them chits for what they asked. I realised I was probably duplicating what had been given them by the officers in charge; but their almost frenzied turn to me, their supplication, their yearning instinctively reaching out to me, must not be repulsed. I knew that in coming thus far, in showing their faith in me, they were taking their first stumbling step towards a return to faith in other men, other peoples. To refuse them now would be to destroy all hope of their eventual return to the world, which return must be made through the channels of the spirit. So I tore sheet after sheet from my notebook, giving chit after chit to frantically eager hands.

Had they been able to weep they would have thanked me with tears running down their cheeks. Many of them, with wonder in their eyes, touched and patted me, still doubting my reality; others clutched at my arms to convince themselves that I was substance and not shadow. They cried out, 'Rabbiner, come to my hut, come to my mother, my sister, my child'. I told them I would come, and in the meantime, if they would assemble quietly near the entrance to the camp I'd distribute some cigarettes.

These cigarettes had been sent me for distribution among the Jewish troops in Holland. But every time I offered them I had been requested to keep them for those we were liberating. I had brought them with me in my truck that morning.

It was a motley crowd of men, women and children which gathered at the entrance, watching curiously and silently as I drove my truck through the gates. I placed the box of cigarettes on the right of the driving seat, and told them to file past in an orderly manner. I did not expect a regular queue, but it was necessary to have a modicum of discipline if I was to distribute the cigarettes fairly. They took the packets eagerly, saying they would be 'for my husband', 'for my brother', or, if a child, 'for my father', and 'for my mother'. Things were going smoothly, and I felt that at last I was beginning to help them. Suddenly I had a shock. I put my hand deeper into the box, but could not feel any more cigarettes. I turned sharply, and saw that the box was almost empty. How could this have happened? I knew I had so far distributed only about a quarter of its contents. I turned round on them in anger: 'Someone has been stealing the cigarettes!' The upturned faces were expressionless. 'Who has taken them? Tell me, who did this?' They continued to stare at me mutely, incomprehensibly. In my mind's eye I saw they had taken cigarettes from my hand on one side, and then had walked round to the other side and dipped into the box behind me. I felt annoyed with myself, and my anger mounted. 'Tell me this instant or you'll get no more!' They continued to stare at me in unresponsive silence. 'Stand away! that's enough!' I drove the truck out through the gates, alighted, and re-entered the camp; they had not stopped to watch or to wait for me, they had simply melted away. Thinking it over afterwards, I knew I was wrong; I had expected some observance of law and order – it was much too soon for that.

*   *   *

Kramer's dining-room had been taken over as the officers' mess. There I found my fellow officers, who expressed their sympathy and shock at what they were witnessing. They were bewildered at some of the reactions shown by the inmates. I begged them, 'Be patient; these people are not just sick recovering from an illness; they have not just been pardoned for any crime or holding some political idea. These are people who have been herded together for weeks, months, and some even for years, and subjected to physical, mental and spiritual torture and debasement more sadistic than anything in human experience. They have been subjected not only to a deliberate extermination of themselves as a people, but to a disintegration of their souls. They have become, not outcasts of society, but outcasts of Life. You are trained to war, and you know what war can do: the devastation, the destruction, the blood, the raw, gaping wounds of war – these you know; you can face up to them,

19

you can deal with them. But here is something different, beyond your ken, and beyond mine also.'

My fellow officers listened with quiet attention.

'In this morass of human misery you are bringing alleviation to many who are beyond it. They are grateful for the liberation you've brought them, but it's still too recent for them to understand it. You want to help them; but they are unco-operative, and your discipline and orders are being met with apathy and suspicion.

'Be patient, as I, too, must be patient with them.

'They will bring you "chits" signed by me for many things which you have already authorised. Don't be angry with them, but use your discretion. At the moment they're like children; they have no sense of proportion, and their hunger for every kind of material good is terrible. There is also another kind of good – an abstract one, but just as necessary, and I feel at the moment only I can supply that.'

I was immensely cheered with my fellow officers' immediate response. One of them offered to accompany me on a visit to the huts, and we went together.

We entered one of the worst of the women's huts, and we saw hundreds of women who I at first thought were all middle aged, or old. They were lying on the floor, or on one another in filth and dirt, even in their own excrement, not having the strength to clean themselves. Lice were swarming all over the place. Among them were many dead, and these were being used as pillows and mattresses. Later, in the presence of a high-ranking medical officer the hut was measured, and we found that twenty people were forced to sleep within the space allotted to one British soldier.

My presence in the camp had come to the knowledge even of these wretched women, whose link with life was now only a thread; even as we stood there we heard the rattle of death, followed by a thin, piercing cry, 'Mama, don't die, don't leave me!'

Through dried, parched lips, in a bird-like squeak, they called to me, 'Rabbiner, save me; food, a piece of white bread; my child is dying. Rabbiner, save my mother; save my sister, she is all I have left of a family of twenty. Rabbiner, dysentery; save me.' The sight and sound of this awful misery pierced my heart. My fellow officer asked me, 'What are they saying?' I told him, and added, 'You are fortunate that you don't understand the language; it makes it easier for you.'

'We are distributing soup, and water and sugar to the worst cases,' he told me. 'But I'm afraid it's too late; most of them will die.'

'They need urgent medical attention; they should be sent to hospital.'

He shook his head. 'There's still a war on, you know. I can't see what you can do for them, Padre, except perform the last rites.'

'Where there's the very least hope of saving a life I want to help and try to save that life.'

'Don't you think it might be more merciful if most of them died? If their lives are saved, will they return to the world as normal people?' He spoke with frank sincerity.

'That depends so much on us,' I replied. 'In saving them we're showing them that we want them, that they are not outcasts – if we can do this, then we're making amends, small though they may be, for the evil that has been done to them; we are the instruments of the first repudiation, no matter how tardy, or how small.'

'But will they not remember this all their lives?'

'I dare say they will; but if they can know and remember also the miracle of their liberation, and their return to the world as a free people, then the memory of this inferno will in time fade before the dawn of deliverance. We can never eradicate the scars; but as medicine heals the body, so must faith heal the soul.'

That afternoon we visited other huts. In many of them

c

the story was the same: dirt, disease, dying and dead all packed together. The Unit had ordered every hut to appoint its own 'overseer' to act as a liaison between them and the various officers. The new authorities were anxious to have the dead removed from the huts, and under the instruction of the 'overseer' this was now being done. But only very slow progress was being made, for the inmates were too apathetic, and were too used to the dead to care whether they remained or not. However, slowly, feebly, and reluctantly, they were gradually removing the dead from their midst.

At one of the men's huts, where its occupants were in somewhat better shape, I studied its 'overseer' in some surprise. He was, I thought, in his early thirties; although his frame was sparse his build was stocky; in normal life he must have been thick-set. When I asked him, he told me his name was Yankel. 'You give me an impression of strength,' I told him. 'The others are all so weak, but not you; why is that? Have you only recently been imprisoned?'

'Not as recently as some; certainly not as long as others. There are some who have been incarcerated here for as long as six years.'

'How have you managed to keep your strength?'

'I was determined to remain strong; I made up my mind that, whatever happened, I would be strong. They took me from my wife, and I live for the day when I can return to her. Then she will need me, and I must be strong for her. I don't know how I should have been if I'd remained here much longer; but now the liberation has come, and I want to find her. Perhaps you can help me, Rabbi.'

I took details of himself and his wife as I did of many, many others. That day I began to fill sheet after sheet with names, addresses, relationships, all the information they could give me of kith and kin who might be traced. The information was often scrappy, barely sufficient to start enquiries; but I wrote it all down, I would not ignore the slightest item which might form a link between one or other of them and some relative or friend, close or distant, near at hand or in some far corner of the world.

Of the hundreds of requests and supplications I received, one of the strangest came that afternoon. It was from two Polish girls. They told me they were in their early twenties, and had been university student friends. I asked them, 'Can I do something for you?'

Sadly they shook their heads. 'No, there is nothing you can do for us.'

'Would you like to write to someone? Is there someone I might help you to find?'

'No, there is no one, we have no one left. Why did you come and save us? It would have been better if we'd been left to die.'

'You are both young, you have your life still before you. Let me help you.'

'No there's nothing you can do for us.' In their bereft and lonely state they were inconsolable, and I sadly moved away.

'Rabbi – please . . .' I turned back.

'There is something you can do.'

'What is it?'

'Bring us Steinbeck.'

'John Steinbeck? What can he do for you?'

'He can write what is in our minds. You can write and describe what you see in this camp, but only Steinbeck can write of what is in here,' touching their foreheads with significant fingers.

Long afterwards that strange plea echoed in my memory. That anguished plea which humbled me then, as it does now, for it showed me that in their desolation they still retained culture.

And then I found Rabbi Olefsky, a young Polish rabbi aged twenty-six. When he was sent to Belsen he brought with him in his mind the entire Babylonian Talmud, which he had learned by heart; and every day he spent in Belsen he forced himself to con a portion in his memory. The Nazis could never kill the innate culture of the Jew.

I received word that the burial squad had completed their operations for the day, and I made my way back to the grave. The huge pile of bodies was gone, buried in this earthy pit, offensive no longer to man's eye, but only to his memory. I looked down on the freshly turned soil, and mentally beneath it saw 5,000 mutilated, mangled lives.

The Protestant padre and the officer in charge were waiting for me at the graveside. I asked my fellow padre if he would like to say the first prayers; but he said it would be more fitting if I did so, as most of the dead were Jewish.

And so, with bursting heart, the salt tears coursing down my cheeks, I said the prayers for the dead. It is the custom of the Jews to keep their heads covered when in prayer, and by keeping their heads covered also, my two companions showed their respect for my people and for me. Then the Protestant padre said his prayers, and the three of us stood with bowed, uncovered heads.

As we left the grave I was still crying, and my companions, too, were deeply moved. My fellow padre turned to me, saying, 'There is very little I can do here. Most of the people are Jewish, and I cannot talk even with those of my faith, as I do not know the language. You are needed, you must stay.'

As the day drew to a close I was once more worn out, but I remained in the camp until after nightfall. The moon rose and touched it with silver. All who could walk came out of their huts to share the stillness, the kindness, and the freedom of the night. Beneath the gentle light of the moon the outlines of the camp were less harsh, and one lost one's identity, becoming only movement and voice, merging with the darkness.

We sat on the ground in a large semi-circle, and sang songs. Among us was a young Lithuanian woman named

Sima, who had been an actress and a singer, and who had a song she wished to sing. It had been composed by a friend who had been with her in the Estonian camp. One day he had decided to escape, and before going had given her the manuscript. She had torn it up and hidden it on her person, and on the day of liberation the first thing she had done was to put the pieces together. She showed me the manuscript. It was called 'The Partisan Song', and was signed 'Herschel Glick'. She stood up and began to sing, and the others joined in with her:

Never say this is to be your last adieu,
When benighted days obscure the vault of blue:
The long-awaited hour surely will appear,
As defiantly our step will stamp 'We're here'.

From land of verdant palms to regions white with snow,
We're here, anguish-ridden, yea! borne down with woe;
But where'er a drop of Jewish blood did spurt
There will sprout anew our ancient grit and spirit.

The morning sun afresh will gild for us our 'now',
As wretched yesterday will vanish with the foe;
And if the dawn is late in coming through the sun,
Then must this song – a watchword – pass from sire to son.

This battle-song in blood instead of ink we write.
No, 'tis not a skylark's lilt in carefree flight;
Midst tumbling walls a people grimly takes its stand,
And proclaims its boding message, gun in hand.

Then never say this is to be your last adieu,
When benighted days obscure the vault of blue;
The long awaited hour surely will appear,
As defiantly our step will stamp 'We're here'.

How well I remember those voices. They all had a flat, metallic tone, and it was strange to hear women, from whom one expects soft or high pitched voices, emitting sounds which might have come from the throats of tin men.

I remember two sisters, Shoshanna and Esta, who sang 'Whither Shall We Go?'* Some years later I was to hear that same song sung by a well-known variety artist, and I was immediately carried back to the unforgettable moment when first I heard it. Through the nostalgic notes of the professional singer came the tinny voices of Shoshanna and Esta.

Afterwards Sima talked to me about Herschel Glick. He was born in Vilna, belonged to the Writers' Group, and in 1942 won the Literature prize in the Vilna Ghetto. It was there he composed the Partisan Song. He also wrote prose foretelling the ultimate destruction of the Nazis, and a satire on the German soldier at the front, in which the soldier wrote home to his sweetheart that the Germans were being beaten and driven back, that the once smart and methodical soldiers were looking like tramps, that some had even lost their trousers and were completely dishevelled and undignified. After this, Glick was called the Young Prophet.

I can still hear Sima's voice saying, 'He wasn't a big man, not more than five feet six inches tall, and very slight. We all loved him, he was so thoughtful and considerate of others. He came into the Estonian Camp from the Vilna Ghetto.'

'Wasn't that liquidated?'

'Yes, but not before a group of partisans decided to fight to the death. Glick was one of these; he made hand grenades, but was caught and sent to Estonia.'

'That may have saved his life.'

'Only for a time. The camp in Estonia was on the banks of the river Narva. The non-Jewish population was sympathetic to the Jewish internees, and often gave them food. ~

* A well-known Yiddish folk song, expressing the Jew's lack of a homeland.

26

Glick used to go out, and one day he brought back several tomatoes, and gave me one. That was how we became friends.'

'When did you last see him?' I asked.

'In 1944, in August. He came to me and said, "Our turn to be shot is nearing, let us escape." But I could not go; my husband was working outside the camp, I couldn't leave him.'

'But Glick went?'

'Yes. Forty of them, men and women, escaped through a tunnel. The following morning the SS leader came in and found his cook had gone; she was one of the escapees. He ordered a roll call, and after much fruitless questioning he telephoned the Gestapo, who ordered the forest to be searched with dogs.'

'What happened?'

'I don't know. The next day the rest of us were taken to be shot, but on the road a dispatch rider of the German Army stopped the SS leader and handed him a piece of paper. The waggons were turned round towards the port of Tallin, and then I thought we were all to be drowned. But we were herded on to the ships with our guards, and eventually landed in Germany. Before we were taken to Belsen we were told, "You are going where the other Jews are." We broke out into song, singing our patriotic melodies, including Glick's "When we go on our last journey". After a terrible journey of three days without food or water we were made to walk four miles to this camp. We were brought in by the gate near the crematorium, near the huge pile of shoes, thousands of shoes. We had nothing, we had been ordered to burn all our belongings – we had nothing but our faith and our songs.'

'But you did not lose faith?'

'I conducted a Chanukah service* here in this camp. The

* The service of lighting the eight candles, observed by every Jewish household to commemorate the victory of the Maccabees (cir. 165 B.C.E.).

SS women screamed at me, "How can you retain your faith? Do you really believe it will help you, or that you will be able to enjoy it later on? You will die here." But you see they were wrong. Many of us have died, and Glick may have died too, but his songs will live.'

CHAPTER FOUR

YANKEL, AND OTHERS

As DAY SUCCEEDED DAY I had difficulty in distinguishing one from another. I was wholly occupied with the immense task that destiny had sent me, and I had become so absorbed in it that I was no longer conscious of the succession of days, only of the perpetuity of the problems. There was the problem of water.

A few days before the liberation the SS had damaged the water mains, and when the British entered they found that the only supply was one tank of water, used by the prisoners for drinking, bathing, and washing. It was essential that water be brought to the camp immediately, and it would be some days before the Royal Engineers could help us.

The initial water supply was provided by a convoy of water carts which arrived together with food. This was supplemented and later replaced by water pumped to the camp by German civilian fire brigades, working under military direction and supervision.

When it was decided that the local fire brigade must be called upon to assist, two British officers went to Celle and contacted the German brigade there. They were not received with any degree of pleasure, and only when they declared that 60,000 Germans were in a desperate plight could they prevail on the brigade to come. However, that same morning two chief officers, several men, and two engines of the fire brigade arrived at the camp. They stayed the whole day, but they said they would not come again, as they were civilians and could not be compelled. Nevertheless they came each day until the Royal Engineers arrived. They were told that if they did not come their wives and children would have to, and this was sufficient to persuade them that it was advisable to come themselves; they did not wish their families to be brought into contact with the hell their compatriots had made.

When R.E.M.E. came in the emergency system consisted of two small capacity fire pumps drawing from the river and delivering into a basin in Camp No..1. From this point two similar pumps distributed water to the cookhouse and ablution stands. The whole system was connected by fire-hose. Additional hose and ablution equipment was brought in from the fire brigade at Celle, which enabled the existing layout to be extended, and by midday on April 19th there was a supply to all cookhouses, and a considerable increase in the number of ablution points.

On April 23rd, a permanent German fire-fighting and water-pumping force was brought in and established in the camp. The equipment consisted of two large tenders with self-contained pumps, and one small tender. The original emergency supply consisted of water straight from the stream, and there had been no time to chlorinate or filter it. As conditions improved it became possible to treat the water adequately, although dead bodies were frequently found in the reservoirs.

I suffered an attack of dysentery which brought the water problem acutely home to me. I was asked to go to one of the blocks to observe *kiddush* on Friday evening; this is the sanctification of the entry of the Sabbath, usually performed by saying a prayer over a goblet of wine; so I said the prayer over a piece of bread. I was pressed to stay for the evening 'meal'. This consisted of a concoction made to represent *gefilte fisch*, a traditional Jewish dish. Although rather reluctant to eat of the food they offered, I did not wish to offend my hosts, so I ate, and also drank some beverage they had made. The following night I suffered excruciating pains, and was extremely ill. The next morning someone came to look for me, and he went for the Medical Officer, who called and gave me some tablets. I lay for nearly forty-eight hours before I was able to move. Then I felt better, but terribly weak; and for several days after that it was an effort to get about.

The huts remained filthy for some time, as their inmates had no inclination to clean them. Death was still too frequent a visitor for them to be concerned about cleanliness. I tried hard to persuade, even to goad them into doing more for themselves; but people whose will to live was at an ebb, and who saw more of death than life, had no reserves upon which they could call.

It seemed that the death rate would never be checked; and when a man still squatting on his haunches died in front of me, I threw up my hands and exclaimed in a paraphrase of the 121st Psalm:

'I lift up mine eyes unto the hills; whence will my help come?'

*   *   *

The bulldozer had been at work again, and at the far end of the camp another mass grave had been dug to contain 5,000 bodies, and five or six graves to contain a thousand bodies each. Again I pleaded for reverence, and the bodies for the smaller mass graves were taken to the edge on lorries; then the SS were made to take them down one by one, and lay them side by side in their last resting place. Once again the soil covered the bodies with its kindly blanket, and once again the sun gently warmed the nape of my neck as I stood with bowed head, committing their remains to nature, and their souls to God.

In order to be always at hand I had moved from Celle, and was now staying at one of the houses outside the camp. In the camp itself I had been given the use of a small room which served me as an office. Here hundreds of people came to seek my help, and although I exerted myself to the uttermost it seemed I would never make headway against the tide of human misery. In my black moments I asked myself, had God deserted me? But when help came in unexpected ways, I recognised the Divine Presence in His mercy.

There was the case of the two sisters whose only relative, a brother, had emigrated several years before to Havana, in Cuba. They asked me, 'Rabbi, will you find him for us?'

I knew of no one and of no association in Cuba which could help me trace a Jew who had gone there years ago. I thought about it continuously, but without avail. It worried me, because I felt that somewhere there was an answer. And then suddenly I saw the answer. I saw the cartons of sweets, cigarettes, razor blades, socks and other items provided for British soldiers some months back by the Welfare Department. I saw the cellophane wrapping the packets of sweets, and on it the words, 'This is a present from the Rotary Club, Havana, Cuba'.

As far as I knew not one of the recipients had taken the trouble to thank their donors, and I had felt this was remiss of them. I had therefore taken it upon myself to express their appreciation, and I had written to the Rotary Club. Some time afterwards I had received a letter from Havana. It was signed 'Maria Gonzalez', and from the pidgin English and the content of the writing it appeared Maria was a schoolgirl who wished to become my pen friend. Eventually I replied, but without encouraging further correspondence between us.

Where was Maria's letter? Did I still have it?

Feverishly I searched through my files – and found it!

I sat down and commenced to write; the thread was slender, but with each word I wrote, hope rose within me.

* * *

There was one inmate of the camp who never failed to give me encouragement, although he himself was unaware of this. It was Yankel. The sight of him going about his duties with strong and patient determination was immensely heartening. I drew strength from him. If he could measure his strength to his affliction, could I not call upon those qualities commensurate with the needs of each day? Always he would greet me with a smile, and I would stop and have a talk with him.

One day I realised I had not seen Yankel, and upon enquiring for him, I was told he was sick.

'Yankel!' I hurried to his hut.

I found him lying in his bunk, and was dumbfounded at the change in him. Gone was the determination, the serene patience, the manifest strength. Here was one who had once been a man, but was now only a weak and defenceless creature.

'What is it, Yankel? What has happened?'

He looked at me with dark and piteous eyes, and in a voice which I did not recognise he replied, 'I have found her.'

'You have found your wife? Is she alive? Is she well?'

He nodded assent, and I felt a great thankfulness. 'My friend, give thanks to God: you are one in thousands.'

Again those piteous eyes were turned to me, and for the first time I saw them unveiled; the man's suffering rose from their depths and spilled over. I waited until the paroxysm of silent tears had passed, and then said, 'Tell me what has happened.'

'Rabbi, I have lost my strength; I have found her, but my strength has gone.'

Little by little I drew his story from him. That morning he had been walking through the camp, and on passing one of the women's huts he had noticed a woman sitting outside. He did not know what first attracted his attention, but something made him pause and look at her. Her hair was white, and he thought it looked like swansdown in the sunshine. He continued to gaze at her, and then some strange compulsion caused him to go up to her. The woman met his intent gaze apathetically, and slowly focused her eyes upon him. A flicker of recognition crossed her countenance, and through her parted lips drifted the whisper, 'Yankel'. He could not speak. He stood helplessly before her, his arms hanging at his sides, and all his strength ebbing away. So many times had he lived in his imagination through this meeting with his wife; so many times had he seen himself taking her up in his strong arms, holding her protectively with every nerve, muscle and sinew. After months of stifled longing and apprehension the imagined meeting had become reality. Here before him was his wife, prematurely old, almost unrecognisable, her only response that sighing, incredulous murmur of his name. She put out a trembling hand to him; and as her thin, wasted fingers touched him, he almost sank to the ground. He gasped out something, he could not remember what, then dragged himself back to his hut and collapsed on to his bunk.

'Look at me,' he moaned. 'I failed her; I'm too weak even to walk; where is my strength of which I was so proud?'

I pressed his limp hand. 'Courage, my Samson; your hair will grow again.'

I went to look for Yankel's wife, and found her at the hut to which he had directed me. I talked with her, telling her about Yankel, telling her about his reliance on his strength for her sake, his confidence in his ability to husband his strength for her, and explaining that this had been undermined by the shock of finding her, and realising that all the time she had been in the same camp, so near to him, and he not knowing. As I talked I watched her carefully, and when I left I felt I had succeeded in bringing a real interest into those apparently listless eyes.

I thought that after the first shock Yankel would speedily rally; but day after day he lay in his bunk in a state of complete collapse, and I began to fear he would never recover.

But here again I knew God in His mercy.

Every day I brought Yankel's wife to visit him, and with each visit she grew stronger. Gradually her eyes lost their listlessness, and her limbs their lethargy. Now I began to observe the marvellous resilience of woman. As he had fallen at a climax, so did she rise. I could liken it only to the resurgence of a flame from the ashes, its pale tongue springing, curling, and rising higher, stronger, fed by concealed fuel. When at last Yankel rose from his bunk, his wife was there to lend him a helping hand, and with her woman's strength to lead him back to life.

* * *

Camp No. 2 had been the camp of a German tank unit, and also Kramer's headquarters. Now it was taken over by the British and turned into a temporary hospital.

From the first I felt that urgent medical treatment was essential, and I longed desperately to get the inmates to hospital. People were still dying like flies, and I appealed to the Medical Officer in charge. He listened to me gravely and sympathetically, but the best he could offer at the time was a first-aid centre in Belsen itself. Although I was keenly disappointed, I had learned to accept what came my way, and to do all I could with the means at my disposal.

I chose the hut which was formerly the SS dispensary, and considered how to get it cleaned up. There were a number of SS women imprisoned in the camp cells, awaiting trial on charges which were rather moderate, and I asked the sergeant-major to let me have two of them to clean the hut. Accordingly two SS women were detailed for this work, and it gave me an unaccountable feeling to see them scrubbing the walls, floor and ceiling under the keen eyes of a British guard.

However, they did not complete their task, as word came from the Colonel that we were not to command women prisoners to fatigue duties, and our cleaners were returned to their cells.

Nevertheless, the back of the work had been broken, and it was completed by some of the stronger women inmates.

When the hut was ready there was sufficient space for about a dozen beds, and, with two patients to a bed, there was accommodation for twenty to thirty sick people at a time. There were doctors and nurses amongst the inmates of the camp, and so our first-aid centre was established. I should have been grateful; but when I considered the thousands who needed urgent treatment, and the hundreds who would die because of the lack of it, I felt that my puny efforts were of no avail, and my cup of helplessness brimmed over.

I was constantly reproaching myself for my inability to remain steadfast in the face of the human suffering which it was my daily lot to see, hear, and share. Again and again I had to steel myself to some new and poignant situation. There was the affair of the wedding rings. A number of these had been found in the camp, and they had been handed over to me.

There they were in an old cardboard box, about fifty or sixty of them: an assortment of gold bands, a few handfuls of broken hopes.

I decided that some of the married women were to come to my office, and, entering one at a time, should choose a ring which fitted. I watched the first one as she stood staring into the box. She picked out a gold band, and with trembling hand slipped it over her finger; it fitted. It would not have been hers originally; her own would have been much too big. But the gold fillet encircled her finger as though it had always been there. Now I was afraid to look at her. I could see her on her wedding day; I could see the love and tenderness on her face as her young groom gave her the symbol of marriage; her joy and pride in her newly acquired ring, which shone as brightly for them both as did the glorious years which lay in front – all this to end almost before it had begun, to end in withered hopes, shattered lives.

She raised her eyes slowly to mine, and for a moment I must have seemed to her as the rabbi who had officiated on her wedding day. Then the mists cleared, and her unspeakable anguish was more than I could bear. My distress touched a chord, and broke her. She fell across the table in an agony of weeping. It was more than I could stand. I handed the box of rings to the Hungarian woman who was acting as my assistant, and, instructing her to share out the rest, I fled from the hut.

A few days later a girl called Eva came to see me. She said she had heard there were some wedding rings; could one be put aside for her?

When I asked her if she was married, she told me she had been engaged to a young man called Choni. He was a brilliant and handsome fellow and they were very much in love. The last time she had seen him was the day before he had been sent to Buchenwald. She felt sure he was still alive and they would yet be married.

I told her that all the wedding rings might already be disposed of, but that it would give me the greatest happiness to marry her and Choni if they met again, and if I were able to do so. I prayed earnestly that such a marriage would take place. What a joy it would be to unite two people on the threshold of life, instead of picking up only the remnants of lives which could never again take shape or pattern.

*　　*　　*

One day a woman came to me with a plea for help. I tried to meet her need, but I could make no headway against the difficulties which beset her. She was almost like a bird, with quick brown eyes in a pale face topping a small skinny body. When she told me she was a German I asked her, 'Why have you come to me? What can I do for you?'

She told me her story. She was a widow with only one son. At the time of Hitler's Christmas Fund collection she had been asked for a donation. She was poor, her only child was fighting with the German army in Russia; what had she to give? In forthright words she had told the collectors what she thought of Hitler and his Fund, and as a result she had been thrown into Belsen. When her son heard what had happened to his mother he gave himself up to the Russians – he would fight no more.

'I can do nothing about your son,' I told her. 'Let us hope that in time he will be restored to you.'

But she did not want help for her son, she wanted it for herself.

I listened as she told me of her predicament. Before the liberation she was just one among all the women in the hut; they were united in their common suffering. Now that the liberation had come she was no longer one of many; she was one alone: she was a German.

To the other women she had become an object of hatred. At first they showed their dislike in small ways, cutting her out of their conversation, drawing away from her, regarding her with hostility. Now they were preventing her from getting food, and she feared further maltreatment.

'Take me to your hut,' I said. 'I shall do my best for you.'

When we entered together I was greeted with an atmosphere which I knew was unfavourable; it was the same unspoken, intangible, but tight bond between the inmates that I had experienced when the cigarettes were stolen from me and I had asked for the names of the culprits. I was up against a barrier which I knew I could not break; but I spoke to them, nevertheless:

'Why are you persecuting this woman? She has done you no harm; she has suffered with you.'

I spoke as gently as I could, although I was angry with them.

'This innocent woman does not deserve punishment from you, and yet you make her a symbol of your hatred, and seek to take vengeance upon her. You yourselves are the victims of hatred, do you in turn wish to become persecutors? If you do, you'll only nourish this evil, and hatred will grow and fasten upon every decent thing that is still left to us.'

I paused and looked at them. There was no response; only a sullen silence. Beside me the little German woman stood watchful and apprehensive as a bird.

I went on speaking. 'You will be coming back to the world to live. Remember that it contains all kinds of people, and we must live together in understanding, if we are to live at all. I know it's not easy for you, but try to master your bitterness; learn wisdom from your sufferings.'

Before I left the hut I saw that the German woman had some food, and I cautioned them against further ill treatment of her. But the situation made me uneasy, and I sent a report to the Colonel. When some weeks later the woman was sent away from the camp and returned to her own home I felt relieved. But I felt also a sense of failure; the burden had been lifted from me, but what contribution had I made?

Letters now began to arrive, and soon were pouring in to the camp. From the beginning the inmates were encouraged to write, to bring them back into touch with the world, and to give them a sense of self-respect. Officially only ex-prisoner-of-war cards were allowed; but it was considered that the writing of a letter to relatives or friends was of inestimable benefit, even if the letter never reached its destination. Many came to me, asking, 'Have you sent our letters, we have received no reply?' My senior chaplain had the courage to send the letters through the normal post despite the regulations, and he was well rewarded when the first batch of replies came through, and I told him of the rejoicing they brought.

When the letters began to arrive in their hundreds, I suggested to my superior officer that a 'postman' should be appointed, so that they could be delivered to the various blocks, instead of having long queues of people waiting outside the office for them.

For this task I chose a boy about fourteen years old. I had met him one afternoon coming into the camp from outside.

'Where have you been?' I enquired.

'I've been outside, walking round the streets; and,' said he, his face lighting up, 'I was not molested.'

'That is as it should be.'

He grew very solemn. 'I saw German children playing outside their houses, but I couldn't kill them, I couldn't even hit them.'

I stiffened at this remark. I had already been worrying over what might happen to German civilians if these people were to get near them.

'What do you mean?' I asked him.

He was quite a small boy, and, craning his skinny neck to look up at me he shouted, 'Haven't you heard of the gas chambers?'

'Yes, I have.'

'Haven't you heard of the crematoria?'

'I have.'

'Haven't you heard how we were dragged from our homes, beaten and kicked in the streets?'

'I have heard that, too.'

'Did you know they murdered my parents? Well,' he went on with a hard look in his eyes, and stretching himself to his full height of four feet and a bit, 'children like those I saw in the street today used to beat us and kick us, and then laugh and spit on us.' He lowered himself on to his heels, and, dropping his voice, continued solemnly, 'But

I couldn't do that to them; I just couldn't do it.' He looked straight at me. 'My Jewish conscience wouldn't permit me.'

This little fellow became the postman. He was given a bicycle, but at this period no inmate was permitted transport of any kind. Every so often he came to me, crying that some military policeman had taken the bicycle away from him. I then arranged for the military tailor to shorten a battle-dress for him. When the tailor gave him a try-on the blouse was too large; but he refused to give it back to be altered. I assured him the blouse would be returned to him, but nothing I could say would make him part with it. Finally we agreed that he should wear it as it was.

*　*　*

One of my happy moments was on the day when the two sisters who had asked me to find their brother came to my office. Excitedly they waved a letter which I had to read. It was from their brother in Havana. Maria the schoolgirl had been the link which found him.

CHAPTER FIVE

A GERMAN HOSPITAL

I was asked to accompany some internees to the village of Bergen, where they were to act as interpreters for the military.

I walked with them to the short macadam roadway that led from the camp; but when I proceeded along the road they hung back. 'Come along,' I called to them. They would not come, they stood as though hypnotised. I went on again, but, failing to hear their footsteps, turned round once more. There was the static group, like carved figures left on the edge of the highway. I went back. 'What's the matter?' They told me. Their brethren had made that road and the toll had been paid in blood; they would not use it. I stepped off the road, and we found the old cart track, and so made our way into the village of Bergen.

I handed over my charges to the military, and I decided that while waiting for them I would call at a nearby hospital. I was received by the superintendent, and I asked him if there were any Jewish patients. He told me he had not noted any, but if I wished he would take me round and make enquiries.

He took me to the first ward, opened the door, and called out, 'Are there any Jews here?' There was a deathly silence, the air turned into ice and bit into my bones. I looked along the neat row of beds. The faces on the pillows were not human; they were faces of stone, with hatred chiselled into them. We went to the next ward, the next, and the next. It was the same in every ward; the superintendent's query, the silent, icy hatred.

I took my leave. 'There don't seem to be any Jews here,' I said.

'Well, sir, this is a hospital for German officers.'

'You should have told me that before.'

He apologised. 'You seemed so anxious, I thought it better for you to see for yourself. There's another part of the hospital we call the "annexe", perhaps you will have more luck there.'

I found the 'annexe' some distance from the hospital. It was a few rooms in a dilapidated building; there were a dozen or so patients; the rooms were dark, the bed-linen stained and shabby; the atmosphere was not one of care and cleanliness, but of neglect. Here I found two Jewish patients. Their survival made a fantastic story. They were two left out of three hundred who had been hurried away from Belsen when the British were known to be on the way. They had been packed into trucks which had been coupled to a goods train transporting ammunition. The R.A.F. came over and bombed the goods train.

After spending some time with them, I made my way to the goods siding.

Here I found what remained of the three hundred unfortunates who had been withheld from their liberators. A mound of rubble was their tomb, except that here and there protruded a leg, or an arm, or another part of a body. On some of the arms could be seen a camp number, the mark of the murderer, indelible even in death. I turned round to find myself face to face with a British soldier.

'We haven't yet had time to clean this up,' he said.

'Can you ever clean it up?'

'It's horrible, sir.'

Yes, it was horrible, but here my horror was tinged with sadness; at the hospital for German officers my horror was absolute.

CHAPTER SIX

AFTER HUNGER, TYPHUS

IN THOSE FIRST FEW WEEKS the problem of feeding the camp gave me many a headache; at times it was my greatest concern, overriding even the calls on my spiritual strength which often left me strained and exhausted, but which, with divine help, was miraculously renewed. Thousands of lives could be saved if sufficient food, and food of the right kind, could be obtained – and I longed desperately to save them.

At first there was nothing but German black bread and vegetable soup: the staple diet of the camp. A day or two after the liberation we found many cases of tinned milk, bearing the words 'to be consumed by January 1945' (four months previously). These cans had been sent to the camp by the Red Cross long before the liberation, on the understanding that they were for the inmates. The Germans accepted them to show their own 'goodness', but their duplicity came to light when we discovered the cases.

It was considered inadvisable to use the canned milk; but the doctors among the inmates were of the opinion that it could be taken without any ill effect, and this was found to be so.

Such was the diet which enabled thousands of starved people to cling to life during those first few weeks of liberation. But thousands also died, and it was vital to obtain more and better food. The army appointed a food officer, who arranged for various farms to send in milk, eggs and vegetables; but the supplies which arrived were mere handfuls against the great need.

I felt that I must do something constructive, so one day I climbed into my truck and drove out of the camp and into the nearest villages. I called at several houses. My reception was always the same: a mixture of wariness, docility, a feigned eagerness to please, a complete ignorance of the horrors of the camp. They would be glad to help, but they had very little to give. They would show me their larder; would I come and see for myself? I did not find one house with a well stocked larder; any reserves of food they may have had were hidden. At the end of the day I came away with a truckload of preserved fruit and pickled herrings.

As I drove back to the camp I pondered on the Germans' remarkable ignorance of the inferno which had been created on their very doorstep. To all my questions they had answered, no, they had known nothing of what was going on in the camp. There had been no stories, they themselves had seen nothing, had heard nothing. The camp crematorium had been going day and night; it had belched forth smoke which floated towards the village and hung like a pall. But they had seen nothing.

The burgomasters of the neighbouring places had seen nothing, they knew nothing. They were brought to the camp, made to walk across the square, to file slowly past the huts, and told to stand to attention at the side of one of the large graves not yet filled in, but packed with a thousand bodies.

They stood there and listened to the psychological warfare officer:

'While we are showing you around this camp you will bear two things in mind: Firstly, we British have provided food for the survivors and have given them new hope; secondly, you must realise that these people are from every country, every religion and race in Europe. The only crime of most of them was their patriotism.

'What you will see here is a disgrace to the German people, but who bears the real responsibility for this crime?

45

You, who allowed your Führer to carry out his terrible whims. You, who proved incapable of doing anything to check his perverted triumphs. You, who did not rise up spontaneously to cleanse the name of Germany without fear of the personal consequences. You must expect to atone with toil and sweat for what your children have done and for what you failed to prevent. Whatever you may suffer, it will not be one hundredth part of what these poor people endured in this and other camps.'

The burgomasters stood and listened. They looked down into the pit of human wreckage and saw something of the outcome of the brutality, sadism and perversion committed in their name. They saw the heaped mounds of earth crouching like huge, patient sheep-dogs waiting to enclose their charges in their final pen. They saw the khaki of the British soldier, the hideous striped garb of the inmate, the white collar of the padre. But they had known nothing, seen nothing, heard nothing.

Stolid, unmoving, they listened to the officer's words; then one of them, a woman, began to cry. Her sobs broke against their solidity, fell into the vast grave and were lost. The groans of the dead beat against our ears. But the burgomasters had seen, heard and known nothing.

*　　*　　*

Some ten days after the liberation my opposite number in the Royal Air Force came into the camp. I appealed to him to help me provide more food for the inmates, and he promised he would do something. He was as good as his word.

A few days later he called in the early evening and took me in his truck to the Royal Canadian Air Force Unit. There he introduced me to the Squadron Leader of Administration, who took me to the Medical Officer, who in turn took me to the Commanding Officer. I gave him a report on Belsen, on what we had found there, and what we were trying to do. He suggested that I should address the officers before dinner. I thanked him, and asked if I could speak to them after dinner; 'Otherwise, sir, they may have no stomach for their food.' A compromise was reached, and it was arranged for me to address the officers 'before the sweet'.

I pondered on the manner of my telling my story; should I choose my words carefully, should I spare them the worst? Should I relate grimly all the horrors that had been inflicted? Their faces were turned towards me, they waited upon my words . . . As I began to speak I knew I must tell them simply but forcefully, with neither evasion nor embellishment, about the incredible cruelty and misery of Belsen. In speaking to them, and in seeing the horror shadowed on their faces, much of my own agony returned to me.

When I had finished, one officer on behalf of his company volunteered two days' bread ration; the Medical Officer emptied his medical chest; and the Commanding Officer handed me one thousand cigarettes, a present he had received that morning from his wife, the package not yet opened.

Later I was taken to the troops, who had been watching a film show, and spoke to them. They gave me their K rations, which included powder for making lemonade, one hundred packages of noodle soups, chocolates, Bovril cubes and altogether over two hundred thousand cigarettes.

I returned to the camp, restored in mind, and immensely heartened and grateful.

The following day I was to have further evidence of their spontaneous and warm reaction to my appeal for help. They brought into Belsen two or three large lorry loads of different kinds of foodstuffs, and then some arrived in their jeeps, to which were strapped carcasses of deer which they had gone out and shot.

I had heard of a farm occupied by several score of Polish

troops headed by a sergeant-major, and I decided to go there. I found them well provided, and I was determined to obtain supplies from them. But how to do this? – the Poles were considered anti-semitic. I realised that if I told them the truth I should receive no help from them; this was a time when I must practise evasion. So I told them that thousands of Polish troops were in camp nearby without sufficient food, while they were living in plenty. My ruse succeeded. For a week those Poles provided the inmates of Belsen with many gallons of milk, vegetables, and eggs.

But then came an order: no food was to be brought into the camp for the inmates other than that provided by the authorities.

My exertions in the field of provisions were brought to an end, except in one instance. A few days after the order, an American Jewish Padre came in, and I told him of the food problem. The next day he drove into the camp in an ambulance, and I found him parked in an unfrequented spot. His ambulance was packed with loaves of white bread, which with some connivance we distributed amongst the inmates.

But still many continued to die from the effects of starvation. On the day we issued the white bread, some died clutching the loaves in their hands.

It was about this time that my Senior Chaplain came to see me. He was stationed at 2nd Army Headquarters, and I had been almost bombarding him with my demands for more food, more medical assistance. At last he had to come and see me. 'At headquarters it's being said of you that you're going out of your mind.' My response was to take him to one of the worst huts. He came out with a face as white as a sheet. 'Now repeat your statement,' I said. But he could only mutter, 'It's terrible, terrible.' I saw him off at the gate, and he took my hand: 'You must stay here until more help arrives; I shall do all I can.'

The authorities decided to call in an expert, who had had experience in feeding starved people. At the time of the Bengal famine he had been sent out to tackle the situation, and he had made a great success of the job.

At Belsen he made a special brew, but the inmates refused to take it. I went to see him, and found him perplexed and despondent:

'I can't understand it, Padre. This preparation has saved thousands of lives, but the people here simply reject it.'

I told him of what I had done, and he was horrified. 'You say you gave them pickled herrings? It may interest you to know that we have made some post-mortems, and we have found their insides to be raw.'

'I am a layman in these matters,' I said, 'but I respectfully suggest that the herrings did them no harm. It's the kind of food they were used to. I felt that the mere sight of such food would give them some appetite. Your preparation may be excellent in itself, but to them it's strange and tasteless; it's not their stomachs so much as their minds which turn away from it.'

'I understand your view, Padre; but I must get them to take the food I prepare for them.'

'They are used to highly seasoned food; if you could add something to give a spicy taste to your preparation it might help.'

He said he would consider this, and he did season his brew enough to prevail upon the inmates to take it; but he did not meet with the success he had achieved in Bengal.

We had to consider also the question of the quantity of food to be given. Scales were worked out on a scientific basis, and care was taken to ensure that not too much was given. The normal dietary consisted of:

2 oz Dried milk
1 oz Sugar
2 oz Flour
6 oz Bread

4 oz Tinned vegetables
½ oz Concentrated soup
2 oz Tinned meat
16 oz Potatoes
½ oz Salt
2 oz Ascorbic acid tablets.

Some of the inmates complained that they were not getting sufficient food and, in another talk with the doctor, I told him that my experience before he arrived was that even the severely under-nourished bodies tolerated quite a quantity of food.

When he eventually confided in me that, in all probability, I had helped to save many lives, I ignored the official order that 'No officer or other ranks must give the people additional food'. I felt, rightly or wrongly, that it was issued because of the army's inability to obtain more food, and not because of any injurious effect extra food might have.

The Medical Research Council sponsored a team to assist in dealing with the appalling state of affairs. In a report this team concluded that the intravenous protein hydrolysates tested were not of much value for treating starving people in the conditions prevalent.

Another report stated:

(a) Digestion of milk and fats can still proceed in the gastro-intestinal tract of even extremely undernourished subjects. It is only when patients are almost dying of starvation that digestion fails, and under such conditions parenteral feeding with protein hydrolysates is unlikely to save them.

(b) *Starving people need abundance of food: they do not have to be nursed back slowly to a state in which they can take a full diet.*

A Yugoslavian Army officer, a liberated prisoner of

war, came into the camp, looking for his family. He found his wife in a terrible state, as bad as any other case. He looked after her, he scoured the neighbouring villages, he went miles to obtain and bring her medicines and food, particularly cod liver oil, orange juice, and the like. She lived, thousands died.

The scourge of typhus had yet to be allayed. The staff of the temporary hospital at Camp No. 2 had been reinforced with additional doctors, and German nurses. The authorities gave priority of entry to typhus cases, all the sufferers in the camp being marked with a pencilled 'T' on the forehead. Many of the inmates of the camp were so desperately anxious to get away from their sordid surroundings that they marked themselves with a 'T', and thus secured removal to the temporary hospital.

Later the American Military Typhus Commission arrived and administered injections, which were about 80 per cent successful.

At last Death stayed its hand, and the daily death rate was counted only in dozens. In Camp No. 1 the last mass grave had been dug and filled, and the burial squad made ready one hundred single graves. God was merciful; only twenty of these graves had to be occupied. Using my truck as a hearse, I took the poor victims on their last journey.

One of these was the sister of Shoshanna. I remembered these two young women singing 'Whither shall we go?' on the second night of the liberation. Now, six weeks later, Shoshanna's sister had died, and Shoshanna came to me, asking me to bury her.

I stood in the soft earth at the bottom of the grave, and the body, wrapped in a blanket, was handed down to me. Tenderly I laid it to rest, and then many hands reached down, and helped me out again on to firm ground. Soon the sun blazed down on the newly filled grave, and the body of Shoshanna's sister rested in the coolness and darkness of the soil. As I performed the last rites, Shoshanna stood beside me, crying quietly. We came away together, and through her tears she thanked me for what I had done. Her voice seemed less metallic than when I had first heard it, and there was about her a new womanish quality. Over the past six weeks she had been steadily recovering; but surely it is tears that are the most womanly quality of all.

CHAPTER SEVEN

'BLOODY JEWS!'

THE AMERICANS had liberated Buchenwald, and from this and other camps people came into Belsen, looking for kith and kin. In a wretched condition, without means, transport, or help of any kind, somehow they managed to reach us. The first intimation I had of their coming was on the day I found a woman lying on the ground in a state of complete collapse. A youth was bent over her, patting her white hair, and murmuring over and over again, 'Mama, Mama.' He had come from Buchenwald in search of his mother, but at the sight of him she had fallen prostrate.

Shortly after this, Eva came again to my office: I remembered her as the girl who had asked me to save a wedding ring for her. She looked much better than when I had first seen her, she had a personal charm; undoubtedly she had been a beautiful girl, and would be a lovely woman. Now she appeared downcast. 'What's the matter, Eva?' I asked. 'Have you bad news of your fiancé?'

She shook her head. 'Not bad news; he's alive – he's here.'

Evidently something was amiss; I waited for her to continue.

'I don't want to marry him; I don't love him any more.'

I looked at her. This girl had known the joy and reciprocation of youthful love, had retained and been sustained by its impressions and memories; love had served her as a cloak and as a light through the darkness.

I asked her, 'Have you told him?'

'No; I came to ask you to tell him.'

'Come; let us go to him.'

When I saw Choni I realised immediately what had happened. He looked ghastly; there wasn't a vestige of the handsome young man Eva had described to me when she first came to my office. I looked from him to Eva, and I understood. Eva's memory of Choni was not this wizened, skeleton creature. But there was no mistaking the look of almost crazed happiness in Choni's eyes – small wonder that in some incomprehensible fashion he had managed to reach Belsen.

I talked to him, but I said nothing of Eva's conversation with me. Later I spoke to Eva alone. I could see she was disappointed in me, but I pointed out the cruelty of telling Choni just at the moment he had found her. 'You must have felt the same,' I said. 'Otherwise you would have told him yourself.'

I begged her to wait until Choni regained his health. 'At least give him a chance to recover; then, when he is well and strong, we can tell him.' She assented.

It was not with any levity, but with a lightness of spirit that I pondered on the problem of Eva and Choni. At the resurgence of those emotions that call forth the recreation of man, I experienced almost a feeling of exhilaration. Here was one of the first intimations that my people were beginning to live again; here was a problem of Life.

As I made my way to the mess that evening, the heart-ache that I had now come to regard as habitual withdrew from me, and a forgotten elasticity broke into my gait. That morning there had been some changes in the personnel, and as I entered the mess some recently arrived officers were grouped with others, and were talking. Words fell upon my ears. 'Bloody Jews, it's good for them.' Someone caught the speaker's arm, but it was too late. I stood as though struck.

Then a blind rage swept over me, and I could have felled him to the ground; instead, I turned on my heel and left the mess. I returned to my office and sank on to a chair. My rage had left me, and my mental agony was so great I felt physically bruised. I buried my face in my hands and groaned.

So this was what it all came to! After two thousand years of expulsions, wanderings, persecution and victimisation, culminating in the most cumulative and intense agony the world has ever known, a people were once more to be spoken of in scathing terms because they had had the audacity to live! What had they done? Wherever their temporary resting places had been, they had asked only to live in peace, to follow their faith, and to be good citizens. They were a very small minority among the peoples of the world, and yet in its upheavals they were the first tinder for its fires. Why? Why? Was man inherently primal, and did he feast upon the Jew in his dispersion, his homelessness, and his culture, as the most tempting prey of all?

* * *

In those moments, my thoughts were blacker than they had ever been, and my spirit reached its lowest ebb. What was I doing here? Why was I trying so hard, in my small way, to restore life and health to my poor brethren? Might it not, indeed, be more merciful if they died?

The world would never learn. Out of this hell a handful would be succoured and would live again. In time there would be a new generation, and as the growth of nature hid the defacements of the earth, so would the years cover the horrors of Belsen. Then it would start all over again. So what was I saving them for?

Across the history of other peoples, the word Intolerance has been written in the ink of Jewish blood; and yet the Jews have clung tenaciously to life, and have handed down their ideals and customs from father to son. I am both son and father, but should I continue to lead as I have followed? In German-occupied territory my people have been mown down with a scythe swifter and sharper than any since the Exodus, and a non-German sees them lying bleeding and thinks it is good for them! What can the future hold when the harrowing present evokes not even pity? Better to let them die and lie in the earth, where they will be safe from the scourge of man.

Wrapped in my despair and my dark thoughts, I neither heard nor saw someone entering. A grip on my shoulder caused me to lift my head, and I found myself looking at the Major. I jumped quickly to attention. He sat down, and motioned me to do likewise.

'Padre, I am sorry about what has just happened. This officer wishes to apologise to you. He had only just arrived, and he spoke thoughtlessly, on hearsay. He has since been taken round the camp, and he realises his mistake.'

'It's good of you to come and tell me, sir.'

The Major looked at me keenly. 'Don't take it so hard. There are many who talk carelessly. Accept his apology.'

Before leaving, the Major gave me a piece of advice.

'Don't get so close to things here that you lose your sense of proportion.'

The following morning I made my usual call at the first-aid centre. The doctor in charge told me he was anxious to get a woman patient to the emergency hospital in Camp No. 2. 'If we wait another day it may be too late.'

I glanced at my watch. Soon the ambulance would be calling for its quota of urgent cases. I suggested to the doctor that we get her into the ambulance when it passed through, and he readily agreed. Shortly afterwards the ambulance arrived, and on its outward journey through the camp we stopped it. The driver and attendant protested that they already had their quota, but we opened the doors, and between us we placed the woman inside. The driver, evidently deciding that to hesitate further might involve him in taking additional cases, drove off quickly in the direction of Camp No. 2.

As I stood looking at the rear of the disappearing ambulance, a sharp 'Padre!' made me swing round to attention, and I found myself face to face with the R.A.M.C. Colonel.

Thereupon I received the worst slating of my life. It was richly deserved, and I knew it. I had used my chaplain's badge to countermand orders. I was setting a bad example and encouraging others to laxity, when I knew very well that discipline was essential. Another such incident would mean my departure from the camp. I received and accepted the full impact of his reprimand, which I felt all the more because it was justified. .

After the Colonel had gone, his words still rang in my ears. I went back into the first-aid centre, and sought out the doctor. 'Do you think the woman will recover?' I asked him.

'In hospital she has a chance,' he replied.

Well, perhaps another life saved. A few hours ago I had asked myself, 'What am I saving them for?' I still did not know, but save them I must.

CHAPTER EIGHT

MARTA'S STORY

A MATERNITY AND CHILDREN'S HOME had been set up in Camp No. 2 and a woman doctor named Marta, a former inmate, had been appointed to take charge. Within a few weeks of her appointment Marta's name was becoming almost a byword in the camp, and I was anxious to meet her.

The day came when I stood in her sitting-room, and was greeted by a small, stocky woman in her late thirties. She looked at me with great eyes set in sunken sockets, and asked, 'Why haven't you come here before? I've been waiting to see you.'

'Most of my time is taken up with burials and visiting the seriously sick. If the Angel of Death would stay its hand, I'd have more time for social calls.'

Her gaze rested on the book I was carrying. 'A prayer book?'

I handed it to her, saying, 'If you would like to have it, please keep it.'

She took the book in her small hands, held it for a moment, and placed it carefully on a table which stood in the centre of the room. She said thoughtfully, 'A prayer book should be the centre of my thoughts; it shall always have a place of honour in my room.'

Again those large, sunken eyes regarded me, and I felt compelled to stand motionless and let her judge me. By general standards I am a tall man, but although I was to meet this woman on several occasions, I was never at any time conscious of my height.

'Sit down,' she said, 'You must eat with me, and we shall talk.'

Our meal over, I asked her, 'Shall we say grace?' I took up the prayer book and, opening it, set it before her. I began alone. Only her eyes followed the spoken word, and her face was hard; but as I continued her expression softened, and we finished the prayer together. When she looked up she smiled, and it was like a shaft of moonlight.

Then she made me sit in the most comfortable chair, and I smoked and listened to her. I had heard many stories, but none like hers.

She had been a prominent gynaecologist in her home town in Hungary, where she had been living a rich and happy life with her husband and two children. Her husband was a specialist too, and together they had run a private clinic. Then the SS came. Her husband, 'the kindest, most gentle man in the world, seeking only to serve and to heal', and her elder child were taken away, she knew not where. She, with her younger child, had been sent to Auschwitz, where she was forced to use her knowledge and her skill not to save but to destroy, not to create but to exterminate.

She had been forced to operate on pregnant women, so that the embryo could be sent to the Berlin laboratories for scientific research purposes, biological *Wissenschaft*, as they called it. Any babies which were delivered alive were taken and sent away for experiments.

As she told her story, slowly, painfully, and with many pauses, I grew cold with the horror of it. When she spoke of the 'live deliveries' taken away for experiment, I shuddered.

Again those dark eyes observed me, and this time they were large with sadness. 'Don't distress yourself so much, Rabbi, there were many stillborn.'

I stubbed out the end of my cigarette, and she waited while I lit a fresh one and inhaled the first draws. I believe I maintained an outward calm, but I felt as though my

59

inside were clamped in the grip of ice. The implication of her words was shattering.

She went on, 'In my happier days I used to remark on the aptitude of the saying, "When in life we are in the midst of death." I have since learnt that it's more apt to say, "When in death we are in the midst of life." There are always pregnant women. If I have died a hundred times as a human being, then I have done so a thousand times as a doctor. I have been forced to quench the life that is conceived and grown in the womb; to serve the "scientific needs" of the SS! I have also extinguished it to save the mother from the crematorium. I have delivered babies only to see them taken away as guinea-pigs; I have brought forth life only to kill it at birth in order to save it from Nazi perversion. Against all the instincts of a normal human being, against the mother-love of my sex, against the learning and discipline of my profession, against my reverence for the Divine, I have had to do all these things.'

She seemed to read my thoughts. 'You wonder that I retained my sanity? There were many times when I asked myself that question.'

After this she seemed to brood, and, seeking to distract her, I interposed gently, 'Liberation Day found you here, and on that day you delivered a woman safely of her child.'

'You have heard about that? Yes, in the first hour of freedom I again held life in my hands. A child was born. There was no water; there was nothing but filth, disease, and death. The mother was shedding her life-blood; I had to save her! In despair I ran out crying, "Water, water!" A miracle happened. Your soldiers came and brought water. The mother and her child were saved.

'But thousands of mothers died: mothers with their unborn children, mothers bereft of their children, mothers from whom had been taken the children that might have been; they all died, consumed by the flames of the Auschwitz crematoria.'

I was afraid to ask her about her own child, but she again seemed to read my thoughts. 'My child is dead,' she said. 'I heard that all children were to be taken away for "experiments", so my child died.'

I was appalled. I could not take any more; mutely, with pleading eyes I begged her not to tell me any more. I looked at this woman who had borne so much. Her body was heavy with suffering; misery and anguish were graven into her face, but two dark eyes eloquent with an unquenchable spirit glowed in their sockets.

I asked her, 'What sustained you?'

There were several factors, she told me. There was the will to win through until the day when she could be reunited with her husband and her son; there was her fierce determination never to let her spirit be beaten by the Nazi; there was the comradeship of the few women doctors and nurses who worked with her, glorious and courageous women; there was her medical knowledge and skill which she used without the aid of instruments or drugs, or even bandages, in secret and in danger, against her persecutors.

But now she had begun to despair. The liberation had come; weeks had gone by, and still she had no news of her husband and son.

'Don't give up hope; pray that they will be restored to you.'

She took the prayer book again. 'Yes, Rabbi, I shall pray. I was in despair, and you came; you have given me hope.'

Before I left she grasped my hands. 'Come again; come soon. We shall talk of my life in Hungary, and of better things; we shall talk of the future.'

When I returned to my office I wrote out a telegram to be sent to Jerusalem. It was worded, 'Your sister alive and well in Belsen. Get her to Palestine as quickly as possible.'

Marta had told me that she had a sister, a pharmacist, living in Jerusalem. I had the telegram sent to '——,

Pharmacist, Jerusalem', trusting that the post office would have the expert skill to find her. I was not disappointed, and a week later I received a telegram from Marta's sister. It said that Marta was to contact the Jewish Agency in Paris, and they would obtain an air passage for her from there. I hastened to her with my news.

I found her strangely agitated, and asked her what was wrong.

'Two army officers have just been here; they insulted me.'

'How? In what way?'

'They came in here, they saw the prayer book on the table, they jeered. They said, "A woman like you doesn't want this sort of thing!" They made advances towards me; I repulsed them.'

I did not doubt her. She had no pretensions to beauty, but she was of magnetic personality. In the first weeks of freedom there were many who sought to satisfy their sexual desires, and morality was held very lightly. The attraction of such a woman as Marta was her rare intellect, her knowledge, her suffering, and her own passionate womanhood burning in those dark eyes which must have been both compelling and baffling to men who could have their pleasure on all sides with ease.

What had hurt her most was their attitude to the prayer book. 'They looked at it and laughed; they jeered at my faith – it was an insult. I told them to get out!'

'They didn't mean it as an insult; they may have felt the prayer book was a barrier between you and them.'

'They couldn't get their way, so they belittled what they didn't understand.'

My attempts to pacify her were unsuccessful; she was outraged at the lack of respect shown to her religion.

I handed her the telegram from her sister, and told her I would immediately contact the necessary authorities to enable her to obtain an air passage to Palestine. But she would not agree. 'No, no; I shall wait until I have some news of my husband and son. In any case, there's so much work to be done here; I cannot go yet.

'And now, Rabbi, I have an operation to perform. Would you like to stay and watch?'

I asked her to excuse me. I left her, thinking of the deep religious feeling she had shown. I rejoiced at it, but it was something to be wondered at too.

After this I visited her regularly, and always the prayer book was on the table in her room, in its 'place of honour'.

I had many absorbing conversations with her; about religion, and about her work in which she could now find happiness and pride of achievement. She would tell me of her life in Hungary, and she would talk about music and books, and I would listen mostly, for I was fascinated by her culture and intelligence, and also because I realised that these expressions of her culture were a palliative to the torment she had suffered and was still suffering. Over and over again she would ask, 'Where are my husband and my son? Why is there no news of them?' I would take her small hand in mine and tell her, 'Don't give up hope.'

She would look at the prayer book and then at me, and her eloquent eyes pleaded, 'Pray for me, my good friend; pray for me.'

I longed to be able to go to her with good news; but the weeks passed, and each time I visited her I felt I went with empty hands. She told me that she looked forward to my visits, and that I brought her much solace and comfort. I know I tried to be a real friend to her, and for my part I learned much from this clever, profound, courageous, and truly remarkable woman.

I was due for leave, and I went to tell her I would be going away, but I would be coming back and would see her again. I found her in an angry mood, and she did not respond readily to my questions. But I felt I could not leave her without knowing what was wrong, and trying to help if I could. 'What is troubling you, Marta? Can't we talk about it?'

'I suppose so, but it won't do any good. The subjects are not pretty – fornication and abortion.'

'What is pretty in this camp? But please go on.'

'It's so strange; you allow fornication, you forbid abortion.'

'We do not "allow fornication". That is something which unfortunately takes place, which is as spontaneous as it is deliberate, and the consequences are borne by the parties concerned.

'But abortion is a deliberate act carried out by a third party, causing danger to life, destroying life, and acquiescing in fornication.'

She turned a stony face to me. 'In Auschwitz I committed abortion under compulsion. I also saved many mothers from the gas chambers by taking from them the lives that were legitimately theirs to produce. Now the girls and women here are becoming pregnant; they come to the hospital and implore me to help them. I can do nothing – I have to turn them away.

'Rabbi, I have learnt my skill in a hard school; let me at least use it for the benefit of those poor creatures who in the first flush of freedom sought to prove to themselves that they were still women.'

What could I answer? Had I not approached many an embracing couple, begging them to desist, warning them of pregnancy and disease? Some took heed, many were heedless. They were free, and love was both free and cheap. What could I answer this woman, who had seen every decent thing trampled in the dust?

I said to her, 'Marta, think back.'

'I am doing that; I'm thinking of Auschwitz.'

'No, further back than that. Did you want to perform abortions then?'

'In those days abortion meant something; today it means nothing; or rather, it has changed its meaning.'

'It hasn't, you know; "arrested development": isn't that how you would describe the women who have survived this camp?'

'I would call it a twisted and thwarted development.'

'The same thing, only put more strongly. How are these women to take their place once more in society unless they have respect for certain conventions, and honour for themselves?'

'By instilling a fear of the results of their immoral behaviour?'

'No, by instilling desire for moral behaviour – and you won't do that if abortion is permitted.'

'You're looking a long way ahead.'

'I'm looking to the future: the best and quickest way to bring these women back to normal life is to look to the future.'

'You still have the present to consider; what of these pregnant women? Are they to be burdened with unwanted, illegitimate children, when they cannot support themselves, when they have no place to go to, when they have never known, or cannot remember, kindness, mercy, or any decent affection? And what of the children themselves?'

'That's a problem which I cannot solve, cannot fathom. I can only hope, and play my own small part. Surely, yours, my dear, is to care for the mother and deliver the child.'

She took leave of me sadly. 'Au revoir, my friend; take good care of yourself. It's not easy to think as you do, but I shall try. Come back soon.'

When I returned from leave I was not able to go immediately to see Marta. There was still so much to do, so very many to help. It must have been three weeks after my return that I sought her out once again. I went to the home, but I did not find her in her usual quarters. I made enquiries, and was told, 'The doctor is not here, she has been taken to hospital.' The news disturbed me. I had not thought of the possibility that Marta might fall ill; my mental picture of her was always as the doctor, never as a patient.

I went to the main hospital and asked permission to see her. After a brief wait in a small ante-room, the door opened, and in came a tall, fine-looking man, whom I recognised as one of the British medical officers. He extended his hand, saying, 'I'm glad you've come; she's been asking for you.'

'Had I known, I should have come sooner. What has happened?'

'She has had a great shock, but she will recover. She is a wonderful woman; we must not lose her.'

'A shock! Bad news?'

'I'm afraid so. She has heard that her husband is dead, beaten to death a few weeks before the liberation; her son is gone too, reduced to ashes in one of those infamous crematoria.'

'Poor woman! May God help her.'

'She tried to kill herself, took poison. We found her just in time. We've done all we could, and she is recovering now; but you'll find her in a very low state of mind; do see what you can do.'

'Why did I have to be away? Why wasn't I here to help soften the blow for her?'

'I don't think you could have done; I don't think anyone could. I know her history; I have seen her work here; I know she's an indomitable woman. And that kind of woman takes her misfortunes on her own shoulders, and responds in her own way. She knew how much she could take, and so she chose oblivion.'

'But God chose otherwise; perhaps there is something for her yet.'

'Perhaps; but now there's uphill work to be tackled, by both of us.'

I shook his hand warmly, and he himself showed me into Marta's room. She lay very still in her narrow hospital bed, and as I took the chair to sit quietly beside her, she hardly gave an indication that she was conscious of my presence. She looked like a charcoal sketch, with her dark eyes more sunken than ever, her short hair black on her pillow, and her eyebrows pencilled on her thin, white face. I took her small hand gently in mine, and it was quite lost between my broad palms. I began a prayer, but she stopped me. 'No, my friend; we did not pray hard enough, and now it's too late.'

There was little I could do on that first visit. I stayed a short while, sitting beside her, hoping my presence would bring her comfort.

I continued to visit her, and I prayed for her constantly, but I did not tell her of my prayers. I felt that in spite of this last cruel blow she still retained her deep religious feeling; but it had suffered a terrible setback. The prayer book I had given her was no longer the centre of her thoughts, and when she returned to her work at the maternity home she would move it from its 'place of honour', and put it in some obscure corner where it would lie neglected and forgotten, until a kinder Providence caused her to look once more to the fullness of prayer. It seemed to me that at this juncture her mind sought only to escape into automatism.

As her physical condition improved I was increasingly eager to bring up the subject of her sister in Jerusalem. I felt it was essential for her to leave Belsen as soon as this could be arranged.

I remember the day I went to visit her, determined to broach the subject, and to persuade her to leave for Palestine and a new life. I was met by the British medical officer whom I had encountered on my first visit, and whom I had often seen since then.

'Your visits are very regular, Padre.'

'I might say the same of you.'

'I do all I can for my patients, as I have no doubt you do for your flock.'

'How is she?'

'She is now well enough to leave hospital. My professional visits cease, but I suppose yours will continue.'

'I shall continue to visit her as friend and spiritual adviser, and as long as I can be of some help to her. Will she go back to the maternity home?'

'I hope so; she has done wonderful work there, and she knows we need her.' He paused, and then looked at me. 'What else can she do?'

'A priority certificate to Palestine can be obtained for her. Don't you think it would be best for her to start a new life far away from here, as soon as possible?'

'You are right, Padre, but she may have other plans.'

I left him, thinking, what 'other plans'?

I found Marta out of bed, and sitting in an easy chair, and I lost no time in coming to the subject of her leaving for Palestine. But for the second time she said, 'No, not yet.'

'Why not?'

'I cannot decide.'

I pressed her to answer me fully, to give me good reason why she should not do as I suggested; then her eyes grew soft and she said simply, 'He wants me to marry him.'

The illumination of thought is swift. It was all clear to me: the constant visits, the care and attention, the slight jealousy (absurd though it was) of my friendship with Marta, the 'other plans'.

I asked her, 'Do you love him?'

'I am grateful.'

I was at a loss for words, so I just sat looking at her.

She reproached me, 'Why are you so silent? Tell me, what shall I do?'

For several days I struggled with Marta's problem:

what should she do? A good and fine man was offering her love, home, security. Another woman in such circumstances would have grasped at it as a drowning man grasps at a straw; but Marta was no ordinary woman. She was still capable of self-analysis which caused her pain, and which made her ask, what shall I do? She could look ahead, and, seeing beyond the present, could ask herself, what kind of life will result from my union with this man?

Of course she did not always see clearly or think coherently. Part of the time these thoughts were swallowed up in the darkness of her personal tragedy. Then she thought only of her destitution, and this man represented love and companionship for which she longed as a woman. But was it enough? It was not enough for her. She had to give, as well as receive. This desire to give did not have its root in unselfishness, for she, who was capable of great love, needed to give as well as receive in order to attain fulfilment. She longed for love, but she wanted love as she had known it.

She did not tell me all this in so many words, but, as she turned more and more to me for help, I could read those underlying thoughts.

In my capacity as friend and counsellor, what advice could I give her?

I longed to bring some happiness to this courageous and tortured woman. I felt I had only to say to her, 'marry him; he will be your husband, friend, and colleague; you will know love and tenderness again; your life which is now empty and bitter will become full and sweet.' I had to say only that, and her decision would be made.

But this was not my counsel, because this was not my conscience.

It was hard to have to advise her to refuse this offer of marriage.

'My dear,' I said, 'all your sufferings have been brought about because you are Jewish. If you marry him you will be turning your back on millions of martyred Jews, including your own family.

'How can you forget them? Their blood runs in your veins.'

'Their blood has been running through the ages.'

'Let us pray that this is the last Jewish blood bath. But it is not enough to pray. Let those who have been saved unite and grow strong, so that never again shall we be so easy a victim. We Jews have great need of you; do not desert us.'

'My friend, I am tired. I cannot fight any more; I want someone to take me by the hand and fight for me.'

'Will he fight for the things you want?'

'All I want is a home and security.'

'Will that suffice, when you don't love him?'

'He is a fine man, I might learn to love him.'

I felt I was making no headway, and I did not want to press her to a decision. I rose to go, and she said to me: 'You don't want me to marry him.'

'I don't advise it,' I replied.

'On religious grounds?'

'Yes.'

'Does religion count any more?'

'Prove to me that it does.'

The next time I saw Marta she had resumed charge of the maternity home. She received me in her sitting-room, where we had first met. I did not know then that it was to be our last meeting.

We had lunch together, and she talked of her work. I listened with interest, uplifted to see the return of her vitality. After the meal I said grace. I had noticed the prayer book on the table as soon as I entered; but I had made no comment, not knowing how Marta felt about it, wondering if she were still averse from prayer. I began grace in silence as I had done on that first visit, and, as though it were a repetition of that visit,

The Rev. Leslie Hardman conducting his first funeral service. The pit contained 5000 bodies. Courtesy of the Imperial War Museum, London. (BU4269)

Leslie Hardman reading the Sacred Law on the Festival of Pentecost at an open-air service. On either side are the Polish and Yugoslav chaplains.
Courtesy of the Imperial War Museum, London. (BU6591)

Colonel Bird speaks before the camp is burnt down.
Courtesy of the Imperial War Museum, London. (BU6671)

The last hut blazing.
Courtesy of the Imperial War Museum, London. (BU6675)

she took up the book and finished the prayer with me.

I rose to leave, but she said, 'Don't go yet; I have something to tell you. I have decided not to marry him.'

'Have you told him?'

'Yes.'

'You have great courage. I should have known.'

'You are surprised?'

'I thought my advice was unacceptable to you.'

She shook her head. 'No, my friend. Your advice was not unacceptable, but neither was it acceptable. Possibly it helped me in my decision; I don't know. When I first thought of this marriage I looked upon it as a great refuge, and had he pressed me for an answer earlier I must surely have said "yes". But the more I thought of it, the less of a refuge it became. And then you came and reminded me of my people, of my sufferings because of them and with them; you reminded me of what I could still do to help them; you told me not to turn my back on my own, but to stay with them, and not count the cost of my personal loneliness. But the more I thought of this, the more I wanted to break away. Then I knew that I longed for love, but that I was giving only gratitude. There followed a flood of memories of my full and happy life with my husband, and I didn't want a new life, I wanted only to be left alone and live in retrospect . . . But life goes on, and we who still live have to go forward . . . I tried to turn back; I failed. It's very hard to go forward alone. I was going to take him as my husband. It was an odd thought which brought me to a decision – you might call it feminine logic. I thought, I am a Hungarian, he's an Englishman. How shall I fit in with his country, his way of life, his friends? Here in Belsen we are mixing with people from many countries, so he doesn't find me strange. But in England I would be a foreigner, and we haven't a common Faith to unite us. Suddenly the obstacles seemed too great – you say I have courage, but I haven't the courage for that; it's

71

easier to remain what I am, a Hungarian and a Jewess.'

I was deeply moved. I answered her, 'As long as you have your Faith, you will not be alone.' I took out my pen, and wrote on the fly-leaf of the prayer book, 'The remarkable courage and indomitable spirit you have displayed during the last six years will continue to be firm and strong in order to rebuild our Jewish nation.'

She read it, then suddenly she buried her face in her hands, and the tears spilled through her fingers and on to the book. 'Oh Rabbi,' she sobbed brokenly, 'I thought I would never cry again.'

She did not tell me she was leaving. When next I went to see her, I found she had gone. I looked for the prayer book in its accustomed place; but it was not there, and I hoped she had taken it with her.

In September of that year I received a letter from her:

'My dear friend; I could not say goodbye. I am so lonely; I long for my dear husband, my best friend, my best lover, my best colleague. You know how I have suffered, you know how I worked to help the people, you said I was good and great, yet God took everything from me. Where is God? I cannot pray, I cannot believe. Perhaps next week I shall go to Paris to get my certificate and go from there to Palestine. I know a difficult journey is awaiting me, and I have so little strength. I miss you terribly and I shall never forget you. Marta.'

In 1946 I received a second letter from her, postmarked New York. She wrote:

'My dear friend: In Paris my health broke down. The chaplain of a Vatican Mission took care of me. I spent three months in a convent, crying all the time, waiting to go to Palestine, without courage, without hope. Then I began to write to American newspapers, and I gave lectures in Paris. An invitation came from the Hungarian Jews' Appeal Committee to lecture for them in America. So I came here five months ago. I have given sixteen lectures

and the newspapers have written about me. I have broad-
cast too. Now I have courage again, and I shall fight, I am
fighting. I have written a book on my experiences in
Auschwitz. I have no money, and I am quite alone – I long
to belong to someone. Please write to me. Shall I remain
here or go to Palestine? I am now studying for the State
Board Medical examination; it means eight to ten months'
study, but I shall work hard. It is now our New Year. I
wish that you and those you love may have a peaceful New
Year, blessed with joy, health, and happiness. And I ask
you, don't forget me. Marta.'

I wrote to her, but I received no answer. That was ten
years ago. What has become of her? I hope she went to
Palestine, because I feel that there she would belong, if
not to someone, at least to something.

Her words still haunt me. Was I wrong in advising her
as I did? I had spoken as my conscience dictated. She herself had chosen the hard way; had she regretted it? I pray
fervently that if the way was hard and lonely, she had the
courage and faith to walk proudly. She had much to weep
for, and much of which to be proud.

CHAPTER NINE

THE CLEANSING FIRE

THE TZIGANE, the Hungarian gypsies in the camp, had made an attempt to return to their nomad way of life by pitching small tents at the far end of Camp No. 1. The day came when they were ordered to go to other camps or to move into Camp No. 2.

They refused. Not only had they been subjected to sterilisation more than any other group, but the frightful constraint of the huts was even more cruel to them than to others. Since the liberation they had gained some rest and tranquillity, and the sky was once more their roof.

Now that they were ordered to leave their tents and go to another camp they felt the confines of another prison closing around them. All means of persuading them to move were a failure; their obstinacy grew with their terror.

It was decided that Camp No. 1 was to be burnt to the ground. When the news reached me I was in Camp No. 2, busily trying to organise education for the children. With me was another Jewish chaplain who had arrived at Camp No. 2 two weeks previously to assist in rehabilitation.

It was midday. Fixed to the right of a wooden shack was a large picture of Hitler, six feet high; to the left, the swastika flag. Twenty yards away was a wooden dais on which stood Colonel Bird, the commanding officer, and two or three senior officers. I stood with my colleague and other senior officers beside the dais; groups of soldiers looked on; scattered among and around them were the inmates. A flame-throwing tank faced the shack. I felt that a great moment had arrived. Time stood still.

The soldier in charge of the tank pressed the button, and a tongue of fire leaped forward and fastened on to the shack. But it was too soon. The order had not yet been given, the soldier had pressed the button in error. The leaping flame was subdued and put out. Not yet the moment of extinction: first Time must stand still; and we stood heavy with thought and waited until Time moved on again.

The Colonel spoke. 'We are now going to burn Camp No. 1. Let it be a symbol, and a beginning of the effacement from this world of evil such as has been perpetrated here.' The loud-speaker, amplifying his voice, sent his words far across the square. Full of portent, they came echoing back to us, seeking out the corners, searching out the hearts of men. 'These terrible things must never happen again.' The effigy of Hitler stared back, voiceless, lifeless. He was dead: had Nazism died with him?

We were about to witness the end of Camp No. 1. Was it the end of evil, and the beginning of good? Should I and others like me rejoice in the burning of the crooked cross? We had paid too dearly for that. There was no joy for us: only a thankfulness that it was over, a longing to start afresh, and an ardent prayer to live at peace.

The Colonel was finishing his address: 'When this camp is burnt down, the British flag will fly over it – the British flag does not fly over brutality, disease, and murder, and that is why we have not yet raised it here. But after this camp is burned you will see the British flag, and you will know these horrors are over.'

The order was given; the soldier pressed the button. Again a tongue of fire leaped forward and fastened on to the shack. It consumed the wood with an avid hunger, lighting more and more flames which darted over the building and seized on Hitler's effigy, greedily devouring it; the hated symbol was no more: the shack was a mass of crackling, burning wood.

The flame-throwing tanks spurted their fire on to every hut, every block, everything that had comprised Belsen Concentration Camp No. 1.

Only at the last moment did the Tzigane begin to move. They folded their tents and took their belongings and left.

Fire took possession of the place. The flames consumed with an increasing hunger; clouds of smoke came out of the huts, thick and black, as though Satan himself were being expelled; and, like Satan, they hung low and heavy, unwilling to go.

My colleague and I stood for some time, watching the burning of the camp. We were amongst the last to turn away. The inmates who had stood with us drifted off early. In the light and heat of the fires their faces were shut and cold. Perhaps the sight and sound and smell of those fires were too much like those of the crematoria.

That night we walked across what had been Camp No. 1. It had covered an area of 1,650 yards by 380 yards, and we made our way to the far end, where the largest mass graves were situated. There was no light, except for the stars. The fires had burnt out. There was only the silence of the night, the earth beneath our feet, the cry of a bird, the murmur of memories. We walked along quietly, saying little, feeling deeply.

I was absorbed in my thoughts. Had we come to the end of the road? Had we come to a new way of life? The outer trappings of the camp had gone; the fire had eaten through wood, had melted metal, rooted out dirt and disease. Had it obliterated brutality and sadism too, or only the events of our limited day?

We reached the far end of the camp and stood together before the grave which held five thousand bodies. I thought of the first time I had stood there, when the mound of human debris had been pushed into the waiting, gaping cavity; when the bodies had been mercifully covered, and I had said the prayers for the dead.

I turned to my companion and saw that he, too, was praying. I must have groaned aloud, for he put his arm about my shoulder, saying 'You have done much, you have done all you could. Thank God you came when you did, and that you were able to do what you have done.'

'I am thinking of those for whom I came too late, and of those for whom I am too early.'

'Think only of those for whom you came in time. No man can do more than his measure.'

'Let us return,' I said.

We walked slowly back. 'It is so peaceful here,' he said. 'It hardly seems possible that such terrible things have happened.'

'All I have told you, and much more which I could not bring myself to speak of, has happened here. When I first set foot in this place, I experienced such feelings of revulsion that I wanted to turn and run. Something other than myself made me stand and face it.'

I stopped to look back at the mass grave, now hardly visible in the distance. My companion, with pale face upturned, gazed raptly at the stars, as though trying to read their twinkling code.

'You won't find the answer there,' I told him.

'You know I feel as you do,' he answered. 'You speak with bitterness because others will not see what you have seen. But these things will be recorded and written about, and maybe they will sear men's minds as a branding iron scorches the flesh.'

We continued on our way. Now there was silence between us, but it was harmonious. No more was said until we saw the outlines of a man and woman in close embrace in front of us. My companion gave them a cursory glance, remarking, 'lovers'.

'You'll see much of that,' I said. 'But the word you use is too idyllic; love is garnished with illusion.'

Once more we reached the scene of the morning's official ceremony. I took a long look back over what had been Camp No. 1, and beyond, to where five thousand of my brethren were sleeping in one great bed: at peace.

CHAPTER TEN

THE SYMBOL AND THE SIGN

I T W A S a Friday morning. I was busy in my office, when there was a knock at the door. At my call someone entered, and I looked up from my papers to see a middle-aged man standing hesitantly before me. He looked fat, but he had been a typhus sufferer, which leaves the body swollen.

I asked him what he wanted.

'Rabbi, could you give me something to eat?'

'Aren't you getting sufficient food?'

'Yes, yes – they are good to us – but I would like something tasty, for the Sabbath.'

I went over to the cupboard where I kept a stock of canned foods. The man followed me, and watched as I took out a can of sardines. 'Will this do?'

He accepted the sardines with pathetic eagerness, and I was about to close the cupboard door when I felt a restraining hand on my arm, and heard the man plead, 'Rabbi wait – please, please.'

'What is it?'

'I saw the Tephillin!'

He spoke with awe in his voice; he was gazing at the plush bag containing my set of phylacteries, which was lying on the bottom shelf. (The phylacteries, in Hebrew Tephillin, are two small black boxes, each fitted with leather straps for fastening to the arm or forehead; each box contains four portions of the Torah, or Law, written on parchment.) 'It's four years since I wore them last,' he said, his eyes fixed on the well-remembered shapes which the plush bag outlined rather than concealed. I brought out the bag, and he put down the sardines and took the proffered phylacteries with shaking hands; sobs clutched at his throat, and tears ran unheeded down his puffy cheeks.

'Rabbi, please, please may I use them?'

I led him to my desk, and placed a prayer book before him, opening the pages at the Meditation before the donning of the phylacteries.

His lips stirred as he murmured the words:

'I am here intent upon the act of putting on the Tephillin, in fulfilment of the command of my Creator, who hath commanded us to lay the Tephillin, as it is written in the Law. And thou shalt bind them for a sign upon thine hand, and they shall be for frontlets between thine eyes. Within these Tephillin are placed four sections of the Law, that declare the absolute unity of God, and that remind us of the miracles and wonders which He wrought for us when He brought us forth from Egypt, even He who hath power over the highest and the lowest to deal with them according to His will. He hath commanded us to lay the Tephillin upon the hand as a memorial of His outstretched arm; opposite the heart, to indicate the duty of subjecting the longings and designs of our heart to His service, blessed be He; and upon the head over against the brain, thereby teaching that the mind, whose seat is in the brain, together with all senses and faculties, is to be subjected to His service, blessed be He. May the effect of the precept thus observed be to extend to me long life with sacred influences and holy thoughts, free from every approach, even in imagination, to sin and iniquity. May the evil inclination not mislead or entice us, but may we be led to serve the Lord as it is in our hearts to do. Amen.'

Then with still shaking hands he took the phylacteries out of the plush bag.

Using the right hand, he first took out the one for the left arm, and reverently kissed it; he undid the leather strap and took the cover off the box; then he placed the phylactery on the left upper arm, setting it against the left side of the body next to the heart; he wound the leather strap seven times round his forearm, and recited the prayer 'Blessed art thou, O Lord our God, King of the universe, who hast sanctified us by Thy commandments, and hast commanded us to put on the Tephillin.'

He then removed the other phylactery from the bag, reverently kissed it, undid the strap, took off the cover; he placed the phylactery on his head, where the scalp meets the forehead, fastened it to the back of his head by a knot, and let the ends of the strap fall down in front. He recited the prayer: 'Blessed art thou, O Lord our God, King of the universe, who hast sanctified us by Thy commandments, and hast given us command concerning the precept of the Tephillin. Blessed be His name, whose glorious Kingdom is for ever and ever.'

He wound the remainder of the strap down the forearm on to his left hand, round the middle finger and back on to the palm, to represent the letter 'Shadai' (Almighty God), and recited: 'And I will betroth Thee unto me for ever; yea, I will betroth Thee unto me in righteousness, and in judgment, and in loving kindness, and in mercy: I will even betroth Thee unto me in faithfulness: and thou shalt know the Lord.'

For over three thousand years his people had put on the Tephillin. He himself had carried out the precepts he had been taught, faithfully and with devotion. This man was devout; but what Jew, even though he has not observed the Law as steadfastly and as lovingly as it behoves him to do, having put on the Tephillin, has not gone about his day's work happier and enriched with the bond which has brought him closer to his God?

Even through the four long, dark years that had at last come to an end, this man had always sought to walk close to his God. In those years he had not been able to put on the Tephillin, he had not been able to practise any of the precepts he had been taught and had learnt to love; all he had been able to do was to pray. He must have prayed for freedom, for mercy, for strength; he must have asked God to spare him beatings, typhus, or worse; to save his family, restore his people; or had begged only for a morsel of food, a drop of water; or perhaps had only called to his God, 'Lord, where art thou? Why hast thou forsaken me?'

Some of his prayers had been answered. Once more he knew what it was to eat and drink, to wash himself, to put on his clothes, to sleep. He was a Jew, he was observing the customs of his forefathers which had come down to him over thousands of years, and in the act of putting on the Tephillin he renewed the bond between himself and his Maker.

The man grew calm, his hands ceased to shake, the lines smoothed around his eyes and mouth, his whole body relaxed. He commenced the morning prayers, and it was as though a warmth rose from the prayer book, permeating and suffusing his very being.

He finished the prayers. Then he took the phylactery from his brow, replaced the cover, wound the straps around the side of the box, reverently kissed it, and put it back in the right side of the bag. He took the phylactery off his arm, replaced the cover, wound the straps around the side of the box, kissed it reverently, and put it back in the left side of the bag. Then he held the plush bag in his two hands, and the phylacteries inside it seemed to nestle within the hollow of each palm.

He said to me, 'I felt that God was pushing me away from Him. With every bad thing that was done to me He pushed me further and further away; but I clung to Him, I would not lose Him, I wanted Him always.' He quoted, ' "As the hart panteth after the water brooks, so panteth my soul after Thee, O God."

'Rabbi, I thought He no longer wanted me; but when you put these into my hands it was a sign . . . He has permitted me to come back to Him.' Gently he placed the plush bag upon the desk, then rested his head on his outstretched arms, and sobbed. His were not the tears of grief and bitterness, they were of thankfulness and joy.

I found myself reciting from that part of Deuteronomy which is inscribed on the parchment contained in the phylacteries: 'And thou shalt love the Lord thy God with all thine heart, and with all thy soul, and with all thy might.'

The man before me was a simple man: he loved God with all his heart, his soul, and his might.

He straightened up and unashamedly wiped the tears from his eyes. I took the bag with the phylacteries and put it into his hands, saying 'Take these with you, keep them; may God bless you.'

He thanked me: his face was transfigured.

I recalled some of the words of Exodus inscribed in the phylacteries, which end . . .

' . . . The Lord brought us forth out of Egypt.'

Then we were led by our great leader Moses, and we were a host of 600,000 strong, a large number for those days. Under the modern Pharaoh we could also point to figures of considerable proportions – our losses ran to six millions. Who was to lead the survivors out of this Egypt?

The man opened the door; as he stood a moment on the threshold, and turned a radiant countenance towards me, I had my answer. God would once again bring us forth, perhaps not under the leadership of another Moses, but through the combined efforts of many. Some of them would be ordinary people like this man, who in his enduring faith and love for God inspired others to struggle to their ultimate goal.

I turned back to my work, and there, upon the table, was the can of sardines. The man had gone. Opening the door, I caught sight of him in the distance and ran after him. 'You have forgotten your sardines,' I said, slipping the can into his pocket.

CHAPTER ELEVEN

'LET MY PEOPLE STAY!'

WE HELD DAILY CONFERENCES at which the officers discussed the many problems which arose, and the means and ways of combating them. It was considered advisable to disperse the inmates of Camp No. 2 as soon as this could be done, but as it would take some time it was essential to move at once those who were well enough, in order to improve conditions for those who were sick.

In conversation one of the officers mentioned this to me, adding that at high level talks it was considered that the best thing would be for these people to be sent back to the countries from which they had been taken. He asked me, 'What do you think?'

The people he had in mind were mostly Polish, Hungarian, Czecho-Slovakian, and Yugoslav Jews: the few French, Dutch and Belgian Jews had already returned voluntarily to their homes.

I told him I thought it a terrible decision, and that in my opinion they would not go back. 'How can they return to the graveyard of their families?'

However, I discussed the suggested project dispassionately with the Central Committee: a group of men and women representing the inmates, and acting as liaison between the officers and the people.

They were unanimously against the scheme: 'We would die rather than go back!'

I spoke again to the officer, explaining the attitude of the people, and their determination to resist any plan which compelled them to return to their former countries. 'It's my opinion that if the authorities insist, the consequences will be serious; death means nothing to these people.'

'You can tell them that if they don't comply, they'll be made stateless, which might be worse for them.'

As an army man it was my duty to be impartial, and I resolutely subdued my sympathies, which were with the Central Committee. I went to them again, and found them in an ugly mood. They were steadfast in their refusal to comply; in addition they were growing angry with me, and beginning to doubt me as a friend.

I had become the unofficial spokesman between the authorities and the Central Committee, and in the days that followed I received only rebuffs for all my endeavours. However, I persevered, observing strict impartiality.

I then received word that one thousand of the healthy inmates were to vacate the camp immediately for another camp thirty miles distant, in order to leave more room for the sick. The Central Committee received the news with stiffened resistance: they would not go! It was a trick! They would not listen to me; they regarded it as the first move to force them to return to countries where annihilation as a people, if not as individuals, was almost certain.

Then a Polish Bundist returned to Belsen after being released and going back to Poland. He was a member of the Jewish Social Democratic Party of Poland, Lithuania and Russia, known as the Bund; they were anti-Zionists, and believed that their problems as Jews could best be solved within the territorial confines of their respective countries. He announced that he had had to come back because in Poland he could sleep only with a revolver under his pillow. 'There is no future for Jews in Poland,' he said.

After my report on the attitude of the Central Committee, a Polish liaison officer, a non-Jew, visited the people in their rooms, telling them that one thousand were to be transferred to another camp. When he had gone several of them came rushing to me, saying that they had been told resistance would be overcome with the points of British bayonets.

I spent the next couple of hours talking to them, anxious to get at the truth. In different ways they all confirmed the threat – or else they had all read into the officer's words more than he really meant.

Feeling between the Central Committee and the liaison officers worsened; a murmurous undercurrent was swelling and was ready to surge into open revolt. If what the Polish officer said was true I could visualise a nasty situation. I sought out the liaison officer and told him what the people were feeling; and I went again to the Central Committee, telling them that the removal of one thousand of the inmates was out of a genuine desire to improve conditions in the camp, and was not a trick.

The next day, as I was walking through the camp a high-ranking officer accosted me: 'Padre, if you were a combatant officer I should have you court-martialled.'

I was taken aback! 'Why?'

'You're spreading Zionist propaganda and trying to wreck British plans.'

'You're quite wrong. I am acting as an intermediary, and my words are the words of the people. They don't want to go back to their former homes. They want to go to Palestine, and nothing will stop them.'

'You're a Zionist agent,' he retorted. I had barely time to salute as he turned on his heel, leaving me somewhat shaken.

The following day the Central Committee sent for me. They told me they had drawn up a list of one thousand names of those who were ready to be transferred to another camp. I should have been surprised at their docility, had I not suspected that the more sober amongst them had resorted to cunning; however, I had no knowledge, only my suspicions. Much later I learned that the list was a false one, containing fictitious names, so that those who went could return, because they were not officially listed as removed.

I was much concerned about the welfare of those who were being transferred, and I appealed for a Jewish chaplain and a relief worker to be sent with them. This was granted.

The immediate crisis in the camp was over, but my own was just developing.

One morning I found a sheet of foolscap on my desk, and, on reading it, saw to my amazement that it was a charge sheet, charging me with 'speaking in defamatory terms of an officer', and with saying that the people would be forced on to lorries 'at the point of a bayonet'. I was so astounded that at first I did not realise the full implications of the charge, and in a daze I placed the charge sheet in the drawer of my desk and left it there. A day or so later I took it out and read it again. I did not know then that an official charge would not have been presented to me in this way; and, having recovered from the shock of the first reading, my mind was now clear, and I placed the most serious construction on the words of the document.

A minister of religion is like other men, but his vocation and training are such as to place him in a different position from that of his fellow men. Events strike at him from a different angle, and the protection afforded him by his cloth is offset by the strong light which is focused on it. A minister must be above weakness himself, but must understand it in others; he must be beyond reproach, but should be the first to forgive; in the service of God he is at the service of man; but he must never get himself into any compromising situation, no matter how innocently or unwittingly; in his desire to help others he himself must not stumble, he must be upright and strong.

I must confess that when I read the charge sheet again I felt far from strong. How could such a charge have been brought? My own words had been maliciously twisted and used against me. I had somehow managed to bog myself down in a ditch of another's making; and if I did not quickly extricate myself I should drag others in with me.

Suddenly I decided what I should do. I left my office and walked down the corridor to the office of the C.O. As I stood outside his door my mind was heavy with foreboding. I shall have to go, I told myself; with so much work still to be done, I shall have to go. In response to my knock a voice said 'come in', and I entered the room.

The Colonel was seated at his desk. 'What can I do for you?' he asked me. I handed him the charge sheet; he read it, and said, 'I have heard something about this. Now that you are here, Padre, will you explain the situation?' I told him all that had happened.

'Shall I prepare my defence, sir?'

His answer was to take the charge sheet and tear it across. 'That won't be necessary, Padre.'

When later I found out that the charge was not official, but a hoax, I realised the respect the Colonel had shown me, and in my heart I thanked him.

On May 24th over one thousand Polish Jews left Belsen for a former SS camp at Lingen, near the Dutch border. They were taken in army trucks, travelled over bad roads, and arrived at Lingen after dark. On arrival they did not want to leave the trucks, and implored to be taken back. The authorities had not had sufficient notice of their coming, and, although a meal was hastily prepared, it was difficult to distribute the food. People stumbled about in the darkness, and there was great confusion. The chaplain who went with them reported that everything was below the standard of life already reached in liberated Belsen. The accommodation consisted of wooden huts, many rooms of which were unfit for habitation, since there were holes in the sides and roofs; there was no electricity, and the sanitary arrangements were inadequate. Within a few days ninety cases of T.B. were diagnosed. The camp was a large

D.P. centre, and in addition to the one thousand Polish Jews from Belsen there were three thousand Russians and two thousand non-Jewish Poles, who before long were openly anti-semitic.

Much bitterness developed, and at first in twos and threes, and then in increasing numbers, the Polish Jews left Lingen and found their way back to Belsen.

One of those who returned was Tanta Luba, and when I heard that she felt bitter towards me, I was cut to the heart; not so much because her bitterness was directed against me, as that she had any bitterness at all. Tanta Luba was the embodiment of the Yiddish Mama. She was about twenty-seven years of age, and although she had lost her husband and her child, her heart was full of the love of children. Nearly a hundred flocked around her, and she poured out her mother-love on them. After the liberation she had been given special quarters in Camp No. 2, and it was wonderful to see her large family nestling under her wings. She had a sweet round face and gentle eyes, and I loved her at sight as if I too were one of her children.

When I saw her again in Belsen she rebuked me, saying, 'You should have told the people what to expect.' Although I felt that no blame was attached to me I accepted her admonition, hoping she would look upon me as one of her children, and would forgive.

CHAPTER TWELVE

HAPPINESS COMES TO BELSEN

DURING MY LEAVE in England I had addressed many meetings, appealing for assistance for the survivors of Belsen. At one of these meetings a woman approached me, saying, 'I have just bought a length of dress material, and half-a-dozen pairs of stockings. After listening to you I feel I cannot keep them; will you take them and send them to Belsen?'

I took the parcel home and pondered on how best to distribute the articles. Noticing my perplexity, my wife suggested, 'Why not send the whole parcel to one person?' I agreed that it would be better to pick out one recipient rather than half-a-dozen. Whom should I choose? I thought of so many; I wished I had several hundred such parcels. Eventually I decided upon Eva.

Eva and Choni were still ostensibly engaged. She had kept her promise to me and had refrained from telling him of her change of heart. While he slowly recovered his health, she threw herself diligently into the work of caring for and teaching the children. Choni was now well enough to take some part in the rehabilitation of the inmates, and was on the Central Committee. Soon he would look to Eva for the reciprocation he expected from her; how would she react?

I had come to know Choni, and to like him more and more. Before his arrest by the Nazis he had been a medical student. He was an intelligent, sensitive man, and I marvelled that he had lived through his experiences. His love for Eva burned in him like a flame, and this must have been

the glow that kept him alive. I wanted to see his face soft
with happiness, and I wanted to see Eva look as she did
the day she came to me and asked me to keep a wedding
ring for her.

I thought, if I send these things to Eva she will think
of it as a trousseau, and in her delight she will turn to
Choni.

So I sent the parcel to Eva.

On my return to Belsen I went to see Joseph, the chairman of the Central Committee, for up-to-date news of their
activities: 'How are you Joseph, how are things with you?'

He was not the man to waste time on niceties; he broke
brusquely through my enquiries: 'What is there between
you and Eva?'

'Between me and Eva! What are you talking about?'

'You should know. Didn't you send her a present?'

'Yes, I did; is she pleased with it?'

'Ask Choni.'

Joseph had hard, cold blue eyes; he had learnt how to
obliterate all expression, so that when you looked at him
you saw only two marbles. I looked in vain for a glimmer
of understanding. 'Joseph, are you mad?'

'If you think I am mad, go and see Eva.'

I left Joseph abruptly and went in search of Eva. She was
sure to be in that part of the building which had been
adapted as a school for the children. When I appeared at
her class-room door the children were just coming out.
She came behind them, holding two by the hand. Then she
caught sight of me, pushed the children gently away, and
drew me into the room. Her face was flushed, her eyes soft;
she was very pretty.

'I'm glad to see you looking so well, Eva. Did you like
the things I sent you?'

'Like them! they are beautiful, you make me very happy.'

'Let me make you truly happy, and arrange for your
marriage to Choni.'

I did not intend to hurt her; I flinched at the pain in her brown eyes.

'I told you I don't wish to marry Choni, I don't love him any more.' Her voice thickened with sullen anger. 'Why are you trying to push me into a marriage with Choni?'

'I'm not trying to push you into anything – or,' I corrected myself, 'if I am, it is into happiness. Have you forgotten how you came to me and asked me to keep a wedding ring for you and Choni?' She kept a sullen silence.

'You are his fianceé,' I reminded her.

'I shall tell him it's all over between us.' She flung up her head and looked at me challengingly; and then her arms were about me, and she was clinging to me like a leech. I caught at her wrists and thrust her away; she almost lost her balance and toppled into a chair at the end of a row. 'You silly girl!' I stormed at her. She looked at me, beseeching, uncomprehending, only to meet my implacable look. 'Eva, I don't know what silly notions have got into your head. I'm a married man.'

She sat staring up at me, with face turned white and pinched. When she spoke the words came chokingly. 'But – the things you sent me.'

'Some kind person asked me to send them to someone here; they're pretty things, feminine things, and you are young and pretty. I thought the gift would give you a glimpse of the world as it will be again for you.'

'Then you were just being kind?'

'It never occurred to me that you would build up such foolish fancies; I can see I've done more harm than good.'

'I was so proud and happy with your gift.' The words came more easily now, but the tears welled up in her big brown eyes, and started running down her face. 'Take it back, I don't want it.'

'Eva!' I sat down beside her. 'Put it away and keep it

for the day when it will give you pleasure.' She shook her head, and once more would have clung to me; but I rose and moved away. 'Forgive me, Eva; I meant well.' I left her there, sitting at the end of the row of empty chairs, crying like a lost child.

I wondered if I should seek out Choni. I had already decided against such a step when I saw him walking towards me. 'I see you haven't wasted much time,' he said accusingly.

'I've just had the unpleasant duty of dispelling some foolish notions in a woman's fanciful mind; I did not expect to have to do the same with a man.'

'Haven't you just come from Eva?'

'I've suggested to her that I make the arrangements for your marriage.'

His face cleared. 'I've misjudged you, Rabbi; I ask your pardon.'

'When a man has integrity he understands it in others. The present I sent her was a wedding gift.'

'I should have known. What did she say about our wedding?'

'Don't press her, Choni; let her come to you.'

'There are times when I feel she no longer loves me. I know things can never be as they were; I love her still, but desperately, not joyfully as I used to. She must have changed; I don't expect her to be the same, but together we could take up living again.'

I told him of how Eva had come to me and asked me to keep a wedding ring for them. 'At the time I didn't have one to give her; but I was so impressed with her earnestness that when some more rings were found later, I kept one for her.' I fingered in my breast-pocket and brought out the ring. 'Take it, Choni; until you give it to your bride it is your property.'

He shook hands with me warmly. 'Rabbi, I shall never forget you.'

'When the time comes for you to marry, let me know; I shall come and I shall marry you.'

*   *   *

Eva's letter came about four months later. I was back in Army Corps Headquarters and was stationed at Plön, on the Schleswig-Holstein border. I had been told of the murder of twenty-five young girls as they passed through the town on their way to Belsen Camp, and I had found the local sexton and made him show me their mass grave, which someone had made an attempt to obliterate.

On returning to my unit I found Eva's letter. 'Dear Rabbi,' she wrote: 'Choni wished to write to you, but I asked him to let me do it, instead. We have decided to marry, and you told Choni that if we let you know, you would come and marry us. We want so much to start life again, and, as you know, it is our dearest wish to go to Palestine. Choni thinks we would do best to go there as man and wife, and I agree with him. I would like to have a family, but I would not bring children into a world like the one we know. People make promises, they say "never again", but I am afraid. In Palestine we shall have our own home, among our own people, and our children will have something to live for. Choni feels that if we marry now we shall have a better chance for the future. I want you to know that I am happy, and that we look forward to your reply. We wish well to you and your dear ones. Eva.'

I thought of those twenty-five young girls, brutally cut down in the springtime of their lives, and I thought of Eva.

I immediately arranged to go to Belsen the following day, then I telephoned and spoke to the Jewish chaplain who had taken my place there. He took Eva and Choni my message that I was coming.

The wedding took place in the communal hall which must have been used by the German officers for their social gatherings. Now it was to be the scene of one of the Jewish weddings in Belsen Camp.

When I arrived in the early part of the day, the bride and bridegroom were going about their usual duties. Choni was assisting with the publication of *Our Voice*, a camp journal published fortnightly; at first it was written by hand; then plates were made, and the publication printed from these. Eva was busy instructing the children. For her and Choni it was not a day set apart for the wedding. Their marriage was something they were to reach in the course of the day.

It was late afternoon when I stood with Choni, awaiting the coming of the bride. It was the month of November, and darkness pressed against the bare windows and gave the coldly lit hall a feeling of sanctity. I felt it would have been better if the electric lights had been switched off, for surely there would have been light enough from all the candles that were burning in the room. It seemed that everyone who could, had come to the wedding. Most of the people were Polish Jews, and it was their tradition to carry lighted candles to a marriage ceremony. Now everyone in the hall was bearing a lighted candle; they stood about in rows and groups, making undulating lines of numerous tapering, pale yellow flames. They were talking in a murmur. Choni tried to still his nervous gestures, and looked up at the prayer shawl stretched above his head to serve as the canopy. Joseph was to give the bride away, and it was time to fetch her. The door opened and shut with the arrival of a few latecomers. A rustle of sound, almost like a woman's gown sweeping the floor, moved across the hall among the congregants, and then was held still as Eva, on Joseph's arm, walked towards us.

She wore a dress of rich blue silk. It did not occur to me that such a dress must have been difficult to come by; I only saw the beauty of its texture and colour, and I remember the pleasure it gave me.

She stood under the canopy, smiling at me with her big brown eyes, and I joined her and Choni in marriage.

At the conclusion of the Jewish marriage service the bridegroom places his foot upon a glass and smashes it. It is said that this is to remind the newly wedded couple that there is sorrow in life as well as joy. I referred to this in my address . . . 'but for you, Eva and Choni, I want to remind you that there is joy in life as well as sorrow.

'Eight months ago you prayed that when death came it would be painless. If you thought of life and freedom they were wild, crazy notions born of your incredible sufferings. Who would have thought then that a day such as today would come for you, when you would be united in the sacred bond of marriage, with your feet on the threshold of the future? You will set out girded with love and hope, and staffed with the resolution to make good your home, your family life, and your rightful place in the world, as is ordained for every human being. After the terrible experiences you've suffered at the hands of the SS, to have you standing side by side under the canopy, realising the wishes of happier years when first you met, seems a miracle indeed! Blessed be our God and the God of our fathers who forsaketh not His people, and Who has enabled you to reach this day. I therefore exhort you, my dear ones, to love and cherish each other, and to seek each other's happiness even more than those couples who marry in normal circumstances. May destiny be kind to you, and in some measure compensate you for your past miseries and sufferings.

'I know that your longing is to settle in the Promised Land, and I am confident this will be fulfilled despite the present-day difficulties and obstacles. With your faith, courage, and determination, and that of your friends, hundreds of whom are present to wish you joy, I feel that everything is possible. Our people have once again outlived their fiendish enemies; I venture to prophesy that they will live yet to witness their own Jewish regime on their own soil.

'Go forth then in peace, and enjoy to the full your new freedom and happiness, and may God be with you always from this time forth and for evermore.'

A wine glass wrapped in paper was placed at the foot of the bridegroom; Choni gave one quick pressure of his heel, and there was the crunch of breaking glass. 'Mazeltov! Mazeltov!' The age-old wish of 'good luck!' habitually and spontaneously expressed at all Jewish weddings, came like a burst of applause. I gave Eva and Choni my blessing, then every candle was stubbed out, and delicate spirals of blue smoke hovered above the black-tipped wicks.

Now the people came towards us, pressing around in their eagerness to congratulate the bride and groom. Joseph shook hands with me. 'This is a good day, Rabbi. It is a beginning, we shall live again.' He expressed the feelings of all. A young man and woman had survived the persecution of Hitler, and were now united according to the Jewish law of marriage, and with Jewish tradition. It was a symbol for all of them. They would live again, they would go forth with their children, two thousand years of persecution could not stop them, life would go on, Jewry would go on.

Several long tables had been placed along one side of the hall, and we partook of bread, salads and beer. At the table where I sat with Eva, Choni and Joseph were a few flowers which had been obtained from a private house in the village. Choni, no longer nervous, looked very happy despite his pallor and still sunken eyes. Eva was composed, and very lovely in the rich blue silk. I commented on it, and told her how beautiful she looked. 'But, Rabbi, don't you recognise it?'

I regarded her with some astonishment: 'Have I seen it before?'

'I made this dress from the material you sent me. You

told me to use it when it would give me pleasure.'

I did not answer her then, and I doubt whether I could answer her now. It was one of those moments that are so complete in themselves; words would tarnish them, and the mind can only recall, but never relive them.

Joseph made a short speech. We raised our glasses of beer and drank the health of the bride and groom. Then Eva and Choni left us; they said farewell to me, walked across the hall, and the door closed behind them. The people began to disperse, the tables were cleared, Joseph helped to take down the canopy.

I went out into the cold November night. There was a dampness in the air, and a rising mist swathed everything. After the harsh lights of the hall the night was shrouded in mystery; but milling about me were the people of my thoughts, and, walking through the throng, hand in hand, were Eva and Choni, and a hundred other Evas and Chonis. The mist was cold, I shivered in the night air. But inside me was a warm glow of faith in the future, almost as if I already knew that a year or so later Eva and Choni would reach Palestine, taking with them their twin son and daughter.

CHAPTER THIRTEEN

JOSEPH AND HIS BRETHREN

In 1939 Joseph was a man of no significance. He had a small business which brought in an income just sufficient to clothe, feed and house himself; he was mildly socialistic in outlook, and took a perfunctory interest in politics. His life was humdrum, he had no particular ambition, he saw only his immediate surroundings and never thought to look beyond. He was not intensely Jewish; he accepted the fact that he was a Jew much as we accept the fact that we are male or female, tall or short, fair or dark. Polish intolerance for the Jew was something he had known ever since his birth; he was aware of it, he did not like it, but he had become accustomed to it; a man could get by, and if he did not think of anything better he could be happy enough. At that time Joseph was simply one of three million Jews living in Poland, most of whom were later exterminated in the horror camps created by the Nazis. He was not even significant in looks, being slightly built, fair, small featured; he could have passed for anything, he was certainly not noticeable in a crowd, his personality was nebulous; in no way did he evince the qualities that adversity was to bring to the fore.

In 1940 Joseph was sent to a concentration camp in Poland; there he learnt the meaning of his birthright; there his mind opened to things which before had passed him by. He tried to escape, but was caught and shot in the leg. He recovered from his wound; but that scar, and subsequent scars on his body, were nothing to the scars he bore on his mind.

When I first met him in Belsen, in 1945, it was after the burning of Camp No. 1, when Camp No. 2 had become a hospital base, and when the plans for rehabilitation were making headway. I was having a meeting with representatives of the internees. Joseph, who was one of these representatives, introduced himself to me. He was a thin, emaciated looking man with shoulders bowed as though in the act of withdrawing from a descending blow; his pale blue eyes protruded like round glass balls, and, being expressionless, gave me the feeling that he had the power of seeing backward as well as forward.

He spoke to me very forcefully of the necessity to bring under one aegis all the liberated Jews in all the concentration camps in Germany. 'Belsen is the most important liberated camp in Germany; it's essential to form a Central Committee for all Germany, with the object of looking after the interests of the internees. There are many who are afraid we shall be sent back to the countries of our birth, and this we are determined to resist. Many wish to emigrate to Palestine, some to America or England, or Australia; we cannot remain here. Our feelings must be made known, so that everything possible can be done.'

It was agreed to form a Central Committee, and I temporarily accepted the chairmanship to assist in its inauguration. Joseph was named vice-chairman, and the immediate object was to establish liaison with the military authorities. This was achieved, and proved to be very successful.

Soon Joseph became the chairman of the Central Committee, and what a wonderful chairman he was! His interest in the internees was deep and genuine, and to them he was a leader risen from the ashes of their inferno – as indeed he was. His efforts for improvement in the camp conditions and for rehabilitation were ceaseless and untiring. He would allow nothing to stand in his way; he brooked no opposition, pulled no punches; he was forceful, determined, dominating. He was no respecter of persons; yet, as the representative of the internees, he won the recognition of the military authorities. Within five months of the liberation he became an outstanding figure in the camp.

He and his committee made contact with most of the Jewish internees in Germany, after which Joseph felt it was time to weld them all into one group under his strong leadership. He had no difficulty in persuading his committee that the calling of a conference would ensure smoother co-operation and would be helpful during the eventual liquidation of the camps; but although he tried persistently to obtain permission from the authorities, they refused to let him call such a conference. They felt that to allow it to take place would be giving opportunities for political propaganda, especially in regard to Palestine. But the dynamic Joseph was not to be baulked.

He came to me, telling me of his project and what he considered only a temporary set-back. 'You can help me,' he said. 'We want this conference, and we want the most important representatives of the Jewry of Great Britain to be present. It was the British Army which liberated us; that is why we ask British Jewry to send us their key men. I understand you will soon be visiting England; do all you can for us.'

It was typical of the man he had become that he had no doubt as to whether I could do anything; he took it for granted that I could and he expected me to do it.

During that particular trip to England I did what I could for Joseph, and went to see several important people, who listened sympathetically, but whose response gave me little hope.

When I returned to Belsen three or four weeks later, I had nothing to tell Joseph but my lack of progress. But Joseph had something to tell me: the conference was on.

I gained my first knowledge of this from the posters which he had put up, and which stated: 'This way to the Conference'. Surely this was not the outcome of my representations on Joseph's behalf? If so, then events were leaping ahead of me.

I found him in the big theatre hall, supervising the arrangement of blue and white flags on the dais. He stepped down to greet me. 'I didn't expect such concrete results,' I told him. 'I am surprised.' Joseph shrugged his bowed shoulders. 'We have permission,' he said in that brusque way of his. I made no further comment. I knew I would elicit from him only as much as he was prepared to tell me.

The conference was a memorable one. It was, of course, unprecedented, unique. There were delegates from England, America and Palestine. The authorities had asked for the names of all delegates, and when Joseph handed in the list he was asked, 'Is this complete?' Somewhat irritated, he answered, 'No, there's one I've forgotten'; and added the name 'Moshe Rabbenu' (Moses our Teacher). Afterwards, when the arrival of the delegates was being checked with the list, Joseph might well have been taken aback when the name of Moshe Rabbenu was brought up, and he was asked, 'What about him? Is he coming?' But Joseph was not disconcerted and replied, 'He hasn't yet arrived, but he will come.' There was no levity in his answer; he felt that Moses was standing at his side.

He threw himself eagerly, indefatigably into the work of the conference. There was no problem which was unsolvable, no difficulty which could not be overcome, and with every step forward he grew in stature. He was now the established leader of the inmates, their official spokesman and the spearhead of their progress. He made a deep impression on the delegates with his lucid, pertinent speaking, his masterly chairmanship and control of the conference.

When Joseph rose to make his opening speech he faced a packed hall of row upon row of inmates from Belsen and other camps. The C.O. and some of his staff, who had courteously welcomed every delegate, also sat in the hall.

'Comrades,' he began, 'this is not the time to despair,

this is the time to hope.' This was the message which Joseph was constantly conveying to them, bringing his forceful personality to bear on them, to quicken in them a new spark of life when their spirits flagged – which was often. The miracle of the liberation and the first weeks of crazed emotion and slow physical recovery had been followed by despondency. They were saved, but they were still in concentration camps. Why were they not allowed to leave? Why could they not go, either to Palestine, or to some decent country, where they could live again? Joseph had explained many times, and he explained again. 'It is not possible to move all at once thousands of people and put them down in another part of the world, dumping some here, some there. Before you can go, these places must be ready to receive you, and you in your turn must be ready for acceptance. Among you there are many lawyers, doctors, dentists, teachers and other professional men and women who will not be able to take up their work where they left off. In many instances post-graduate courses will be needed, and in many more, an entirely new working life will be necessary. We have with us the delegate representing O.R.T.* who will tell you what this wonderful organisation does to train men and women for different trades, so that when you leave here you will be able to earn the wage of skilled workers. You must not fall into apathy and hopelessness while you are here. You must make your hands and brains fit for the new life ahead; you must make full preparation for that end.' He thumped the table. 'We have been saved from death; we are saved for life.'

He then spoke of the liberation, and in eloquent words he expressed their gratitude to the British for what they had done, and were continuing to do.

The conference had started well. Joseph had his audience eager, receptive. He knew his people, he had his finger on the pulse of the meeting.

* Organisation for Rehabilitation of Jews through Training.

Most of the delegates from abroad were repetitious. They spoke of their horror and grief at the extermination of six millions of their people, and of their everlasting regret that they had been unable to save them. 'You must have despaired of our help, but we could not reach you, there was a war between us. Now hostilities are at an end, and to you who have been saved we say, "put your trust in us, we shall not fail you".'

Every delegate was received with great enthusiasm, but the one who was given an ovation was the Palestinian. Standing on the dais, a fine figure in the uniform of the Jewish Brigade, he cried, 'We will not forget you! We will await your coming on the shores of Palestine with flame and fire; nothing will prevent us from bringing you home.'

People rose to their feet, they cheered, they sobbed, they flung their arms around one another.

However, the conference finished on a sober note. The head of the Jewish Relief Team and the O.R.T. delegate both spoke at length of the time still to be spent in the camps, and of what must be done. Restoration of health (many would go to sanatoria in Sweden); education of the children; the learning of crafts and languages. All this and more must be achieved, and would be achieved; and in order to equip themselves for the future they must give their willing and constant co-operation. They must also be patient and have trust and confidence in their leaders.

Joseph brought the conference to an end with the singing of Hatikvah, the Jewish People's Anthem. As we sang, a great upsurge of feeling united us.

If the conference did something for the inmates, it did a great deal for Joseph. There were some who suggested that such an outcome was present in his mind when the idea of a conference was taking shape; but this suggestion was made after the seeds sown during the conference had borne fruit, and those fruits had been showered abundantly on Joseph. At the time of the conference Joseph was not yet a shrewd man of the world of sufficient maturity to exploit events for his own purposes, and even if the idea had been lying dormant in his mind, he was absolutely sincere, and ceaselessly occupied with the welfare of the inmates.

There is no doubt that the conference provided Joseph with contacts he might never have had otherwise. The one-time commonplace member of the local community was now the acknowledged representative of thousands of Jews from various countries, handling the personal problems of hundreds of people, and in direct touch with eminent European and American Jews. They were impressed with him, they liked him, they gave him the keys to many doors. It was not long before Joseph was making trips to France, Holland, Belgium, England and later America. Everywhere he went he worked assiduously for the camp internees, and he did much for them. He also widened and consolidated his own interests.

In the camps he was referred to as 'the little Prime Minister'. He had set up several sub-committees, all responsible to him, and, as no other man of his calibre had come forward, his position and authority were unchallenged.

The black market that flourished in the immediate post-war years soon reached the camps. The authorities did all they could to provide for the people, but provisions were barely enough. Later on, although there were allegations that Joseph had exploited the black market, it is certain that without his contrivance the internees would have been considerably less well fed than they were. I felt that the accusations were unjust, and I recalled an incident which occurred soon after the Liberation:

I had some calls to make outside the camp, and I took Joseph with me. It was shortly after our first meeting, and I wanted to know him better. We were on our way back when we passed a large farm, and he suggested that we stop and ask for provisions. I drew up the truck outside the gate leading to the farmhouse, gave him some money, and told him to go and ask for food. I wished to observe the behaviour of a man who had come through years of hell, and was now about to take on a position of responsibility.

He walked up to the front door and waited patiently for his knock to be answered. The door opened and a woman appeared; they entered into conversation. I was too far away to hear what they were saying, but I caught the tone of the voices, and this was moderate. The woman went away and Joseph waited at the open door. Then she came back and handed something to him. I saw his bowed back and his head bent slightly in recognition, then he came towards me with something in his hands. As he got in beside me he said: 'two dozen eggs', and handed me the change. As I drove away he added, 'She has to provide so many dozen each week for the military; these were all she could spare.'

From that day Joseph had my confidence, and I never had to withdraw it. It was as though during his years of internment he had developed an additional sense, which told him how much could be got out of any situation, or any person; and this faculty sharpened with use. Often I was astonished at his temerity, often I pondered on his acceptance of a small thing; but he seemed to have an uncanny accuracy in these matters. Such perspicacity, added to the hardening and toughening of his character, his natural abilities, and his purposeful outlook, opened a new life for him; Joseph grew rich.

Exactly how this was done, only Joseph knows. There has been much conjecture; but whatever the manner of it, on his way up he never forgot his people, who had suffered with him. That he has reached a height no others could attain is due entirely to his own endeavours.

When in 1948 I had occasion to visit Germany, I went again to Belsen, and there, in Camp No. 2, I found Joseph.

At this time the numbers in the camp were considerably reduced, and, as the State of Israel had recently been established, preparations were being made for its final liquidation. Joseph could have left long before, but he stayed until the end.

He was one of the last to leave, and when he did so, it was to settle in one of the European capitals. Perhaps he should have made his home in the new State of Israel and placed his wealth at the service of his country; but Joseph has become an international figure, and by virtue of his contacts must have freedom of movement, which he might lose once he thrust his roots into the soil of Israel.

The welfare of his people is still his concern, and he continues to do much, but to them he is becoming a legendary figure. He is reputed to be a man with a fortune, and they cannot grasp how such a personality could have emerged from the human dung-heap they had known.

I do not see Joseph that way. To me he is a man who has achieved much, but who, had he been left alone to live in peace, would have been a small business man, happy in his simple pleasures, with a straight back and smiling eyes.

CHAPTER FOURTEEN

'WE SHALL MEET AGAIN'

MY LAST DAYS as a Padre at Belsen were filled with many activities. There was still much to do, but by this time the relief teams had arrived, and two chaplains joined us. I was able to devote all my time to the people, and I saw as many as I could, talking and listening to them.

Mostly we spoke of what the future held for them, and of their belief that the world would not turn its back on them, but would help them individually as human beings, and collectively as Jews. I was of the same belief, and it did my heart good to put their faith into words, and to talk about it with them. Their desire to settle in Palestine strengthened in them day by day. They felt that there they could build up something for themselves and their people. They did not look upon themselves as emigrants; to them it was the last stage of a long and painful journey back home, and now they were impatient to set foot on that beloved soil from which their ancestors had been expelled, but which had waited for them through the long years; soil which had lain fallow, but was being turned now for them.

One of my final duties, and one which gave me immense pleasure was to see a group of people off to Sweden, where they were to recuperate before settling in other countries. The railway had started operating again from Bergen, and the train which came in had formerly brought many of them in cattle trucks as human fodder. It must have seemed a miracle to those who had survived and who went back on that same train, on the road to health.

Before their departure one of them told me of a dream

she had had the previous night. She said, 'I dreamt I had arrived in America, and my sister, who had come to meet me, took me to her home. When we arrived at her house she told me: "Open the door and go in." But I stood, hesitating, "looking for the strings". You see, Rabbi,' she explained to me, 'I had been living in a tent. Then we walked into a beautiful room, and my sister said, "sit down". But I answered, "It's a pity to spoil such a fine chair, I shall sit on the floor." My sister brought me a cup of coffee, and I drank only half. "Finish your coffee," she said; and I replied, "It's a pity to waste it; I can wash my hair in it." When we retired for the night, I asked my sister for my coat. "What do you want with your coat? Are you going out?" "No," I answered, "but I shall freeze without it." '

When the people heard I was leaving, they decided to give me a farewell party. The catering arrangements were in the hands of the cook of cookhouse No. 3, and she went to great pains to make the food as palatable and as attractive as she could with her limited resources. At the party, when we had eaten and expressed our appreciation of her efforts, she came forward and handed me a bouquet of flowers. Somewhat taken aback, and unused to receiving such a gift, I am afraid I accepted it rather awkwardly. I confess, too, that I did not know what to do with it; so, before leaving, I handed the bouquet to a young girl, asking her to accept it.

A day or so later I was told that this had so upset the cook that she had taken to her bed. I went to see her. She looked quite ill, but by this time I knew that the strongest of them could collapse under a psychological straw. The cook, bereft of all her family, wanted someone on whom she could nourish her affection. There were many like her. The objects of their regard – parent, brother, sister, lover, child – had all gone, and in their search for substitutes they imagined they had found a mutual feeling. The result was often a mental shock against which they had no means of resistance.

I wished I had accepted the flowers more gracefully, but this could not be undone. How to compensate her for my gauche behaviour? I could point out that the English were not used to the custom of giving flowers to a man; but explanations, words, would be of little avail. As I ruminated on the problem, I remembered a small electric hair dryer which I had obtained and which I was going to take home. I decided to make a present of it to the cook.

The effect upon her was remarkable. She sat up in bed and clasped the hair-dryer to her.

I saw once again an earlier picture, one of a few months back. It was in the first days of the liberation. A girl came up to me, begging for food. She was dirty and ragged, her hair hung lankly about her thin face, but through all the dirt and misery she was a beautiful girl. I gave her two oranges, and she took them from me with wonder and delight. She clasped them to her breast as though they were two babes, and gazed down at them lovingly, her long, dark lashes touching her drawn cheeks.

I was reminded of this as I looked at the cook hugging the hair dryer. There was the same abject dejection suddenly lit up from within, this time not over the necessities of life, but over something as vital to the spirit. The following day the cook was back in her cookhouse, and appeared to be quite recovered.

I wrote my last batch of chits for the internees in a much more light-hearted spirit than those I had written on the morning of my second day in Belsen.

Returning to the camp rather late one night, as I was passing one of the blocks I heard someone ask, 'Where's the Rabbi?' Thinking I was needed, I went in the direction of the voice. But it was the chaplain of the relief team who was wanted. It appeared that he was expected to marry a young couple; but he had not yet put in an appearance, although the ceremony had been arranged for five o'clock; it was now ten o'clock.

Someone had gone for Joseph, and he appeared. His decision was swift. 'I shall marry them,' he said. Joseph was conversant with the marriage service, and in Jewish law this would have been valid. But I dissuaded him. 'No, Joseph,' I told him, 'I shall marry them.'

This arrangement was quickly notified to the young couple and to those who were attending the ceremony; but then another problem arose. There was a midnight curfew for all internees, and it was already ten o'clock. A celebration was to follow the marriage, and this might overrun curfew hour. I decided to write out chits for all those attending the wedding, so that any of them found away from their blocks after midnight would be acquitted of any felonious intent.

I wrote at least eighty chits, and towards the end my handwriting became illegible. So I was not surprised when next morning I was told that several of the wedding participants were in trouble for breaking the curfew, though they had showed my chits.

I went immediately to the officer in charge to tell him what had happened. When I entered I could see that he had many of my chits on his desk. He looked at the chits and he looked at me. 'So it's you, Padre!' he said. 'I might have known it.'

There were a number of weddings in the camp, and one organisation sent us a couple of bridal outfits, which were worn by the brides; even bridesmaid's dresses were included, and these, too, were used. A journalist who described these weddings as 'lavish and smartly-dressed' wrote under a grave misapprehension. The clothes had been sent in, and the women, many of whom were formerly clever dressmakers and hairdressers, put their skill to good use. There was nothing 'lavish' about the weddings, but it was always the custom of these people to make much of a

wedding, and their spirit now was such as to display un-
inhibited delight that they could once more participate in
a function so dear to them.

Just before the festival of Shevuoth (Pentecost) the inmates felled a tree, and set it up in one of the grass plots
around Camp No. 2. It was to be a flagstaff, and about it
they improvised terraces in the form of an amphitheatre.
Hundreds of people packed together to watch me unfurl
the Jewish flag. As I did so, and the blue and white banner
bearing the Star of David fluttered in the gentle breeze, a
great cry came from them. Then they went almost delirious
with joy, clapping their hands, stamping their feet, singing
Hebrew songs, dancing the Hora until many were on
the verge of collapse. These celebrations went on for
hours.

I did not tell them the exact date of my departure, but
on the last evening several came to see me, and asked for
my blessing. One of them, a young man from Poland, who
spoke English, said to me, 'I am not a religious man in
your sense, but your blessings appear to me as messages
of love and kindness. I was born in Poland, in Sosnowice.
We heard of Jew-baiting in Germany, before the war; we
heard of the paper called *Der Stürmer* and its slogan, "One
Jew less, one loaf more"; but we thought the reports were
exaggerated. Until March 1943, mine was a life of hard
work, humiliation, and worst of all, fear; fear which fed on
the news of the German activities which kept coming
nearer, and nearer. I was one of the last to be "evacuated"
from Upper Silesia. During the march, a number of young
boys broke the column and hid in a nearby barn. The SS
caught them, and shot them down in front of us. But don't
tell your people about the dead; tell them about the misery
and anguish they suffered before they died. I cannot convey
to you what your coming here has meant to us. For myself
I shall remember your messages of faith and hope; and,
although I want to hate, I shall not hate.'

The following morning I left. Many were gathered at the main gate to say farewell. There were handshakes and tears; they cried, 'Don't forget us, remember that we're still here.'

'I shall not forget; and you, my brethren, remember to have faith.'

'Goodbye, Rabbi, goodbye.'

'We shall meet again, my brethren; we shall meet in Zion.'

I climbed into my truck and waved. I started the engine, drove some hundred yards, stopped and looked back. They were still at the gate, staring down the road after me. I had a flashback of the entrance to the camp as I had first seen it, with the sign of 'Typhus' and the stigma of the crooked cross.

Where were the tottering wraiths of skin, bones, and filthy rags? Those I knew about; those were dead. But where was the girl with the brown face? Where were the two students who had asked for Steinbeck, and the ragged beauty who had begged for food: where were they? Had they survived? Where was Marta, that brave and lonely woman? There were hundreds, thousands, whose fate was unknown to me. 'No man can do more than his measure.' . . . But my measure had been so small.

Someone at the gate gave a final wave. I released the brake and drove forward. There was still something I could do: I could tell the world.